THE UNREAL AMERICA

The Unreal America

Architecture and Illusion

ADA LOUISE HUXTABLE

THE NEW PRESS, NEW YORK

LIBRARY OF CONGRESS
CATALOGING-IN-PUBLICATION DATA
Huxtable, Ada Louise.
  The unreal America: architecture and
illusion / Ada Louise Huxtable.—1st ed.
  p.   cm.
  Based on the Blashfield address
  delivered at the American Academy
  of Arts and Letters, May, 1991.
  Includes bibliographical references
  and index.
ISBN 1-56584-055-0: $30.00
  1. Architecture—United States—
  Themes, motives. 2. Architecture,
  Modern—20th century—United
  States—Themes, motives.
  3. Architecture—Philosophy.
  I. Title.
NA712.H88   1993
720'.973—dc20   92-50757
                       CIP

Published in the UNITED STATES
by THE NEW PRESS, NEW YORK
Distributed by W.W. NORTON
& COMPANY, INC., NEW YORK

Established in 1990 as a major alternative
to the large commercial publishing houses,
The New Press is a nonprofit book publisher.
The Press is operated editorially in the public
interest, rather than for private gain;
it is committed to publishing, in innovative
ways, works of educational, cultural,
and community value that, despite their
intellectual merits, might not normally
be commercially viable. The New Press's
editorial offices are located at the City
University of New York.

Book design by MASSIMO VIGNELLI
and HALL SMYTH

Production management by KIM WAYMER

Printed in the UNITED STATES
OF AMERICA

9 8 7 6 5 4 3

Contents

Preface

In my early years as a journalist I had a stern and splendid editor of the old school who objected when my position was not for or against; make up your mind, he urged me, and tell the reader what you think. He had no patience whatever with shades of gray or the complexities that characterize so much of life and the world around us. This is a book that deals with those complexities, not without some ambivalence and mixed feelings, but with a reasonably clear idea of where I stand. It will undoubtedly be misread and misunderstood; ambiguity and complexity make neither good newspaper copy nor good reviews. It would be very easy to take its thesis as an argument against historic preservation and a rejection of the pop environment, and many will—particularly those in the business of promoting one or the other. If that happens I will have only myself to blame; I have undoubtedly overstated my case and distorted by exclusion in my anxiety to state my views. I have no easy answers to many of the questions I raise, but I think it is important to raise them.

My primary purpose is to show things as they are, in all of their shades of gray; my second is to show that they are not necessarily what they seem; nor do they always deliver what they promise. What concerns me as much as the state of American building is the American state of mind, in which illusion is preferred over reality to the point where the replica is accepted as genuine and the simulacrum replaces the source. Surrogate experience and surrogate environments have become the American way of life. Distinctions are no longer made, or deemed necessary, between the real and the false; the edge usually goes to the latter, as an improved version with defects corrected—accessible and user-friendly—although the resonance of history and art in the authentic artifact is conspicuously lacking. These differences exist, and they matter, in spite of the peculiar but politically correct idea that values are either elitist or passé, or simply what we make them. The themed environment that so frequently and profitably trashes its sources is a bowdlerized and impoverished version of the real thing. With the loss of knowledge, understanding, and appreciation we do not seem to know or care when the merchandise is shoddy.

This is a book about that unreal America and how it is changing what and how we build. The most serious, beautiful, and innovative architecture is increasingly isolated—even rejected—for the environment as entertainment, or nostalgia, or never-never land. An architectural breakthrough of singular aesthetic and historical significance is taking place today, and this book is about that, too. After modernism, after postmodernism, architecture is reinventing itself as a great and timeless art. The gap between the public and the most advanced forms of art is eternal; but never before has the lowest common demominator been so enshrined, institutionalized, and popularized in its place, so widely disseminated and so skillfully sold on such a major scale.

Real architecture has little place in the unreal America. A public increasingly addicted to fakes and fantasies is unprepared and unwilling to understand the unfamiliar and, often, admittedly difficult new work, although its complexities answer to the contemporary condition. Instead of a public architecture, or an architecture integrated into life and use, we have "trophy" buildings by "signature" architects, like designer clothes. Our cities, shattered by change, victimized by economics, are still the rich containers of our collective culture, the record of our continuity, the repository of the best we have produced. But themed parodies pass for places now, serving as the new planning and design models even as real places with their full freight of art and memories are devalued and destroyed.

I have nothing against illusion; it is the stuff of our hopes and dreams, and one of architecture's most potent tools. It is also, in this country, an industry, a profit-making enterprise of unprecedented popular success and very shallow dimensions. It has created what one astute observer of the American cityscape, John M. Findlay, calls "magic lands";[1] the Magic Kingdom has become an urban design model, and themed residential complexes are built around a "lifestyle" for a designated demographic group. Illusion fuels the theme parks and historic preservation that cater to the tourism that has become a major part of the national economy. It is the commodity used to fill the vacuum of imagination and ideas when commercial expediency builds to the bottom line. It sets the agenda when memory fails and the world has to be reinvented to hold our attention. But illusion at this level, in the words of the historian John R. Stilgoe, who writes brilliantly about the American landscape, is "tawdry and ephemeral magic" at best.

I JOHN M. FINDLAY, *Magic Lands: Western Cityscapes and American Culture After 1940* (Berkeley: University of California Press, 1992).

I have fought long and hard for preservation, as those who have followed my work must know. My concerns now have to do with its success, not its failure: how history and places are transformed by the gloss of wishful and artful illusion, how image is revised and authenticity compromised to suit the taste of the time. With the best intentions, we turn real history and the places where it was made into selective stage sets, and we find extraordinary rationales for the process. The latest scholarly fashion is for "interpretation," which promotes the use of previously neglected or newly researched documentation but also permits subjective preferences in the seductive guise of greater objectivity. There may be less guesswork, but there is no less manipulation of the past. One faces a dilemma peculiar to the very process of preservation: in saving the thing, the thing is lost and a substitute provided; the past is as evanescent and irretrievable as time itself.

I love the serendipitous, temporal, funky reality of the pop world; it leavens the "straight" scene with its instant, on-target commentary. I have always delighted in the wit, conscious and unconscious, of today's vernacular and idiosyncratic structures; their lively immediacy provides cultural truths and aesthetic surprises that could never be duplicated in the studio or by any formal plan. In a word, and in the argument of this book, they are real, and that matters. The landmarks of my favorite Massachusetts vacation route always included Violet's Lounge, a tiny lavender shack wedged tightly, like some wayward Siamese twin, into the equally tiny and decorous landmark house of a proper early New England poet. The name, in silver sparkle, suggested the possibility of modestly glittering nights. I felt a real sense of loss when that duo was divided and Violet disappeared.

Like so many, I am deeply indebted to John Brinckerhoff Jackson's original and insightful observations about the true nature of the twentieth-century American landscape and the products of popular taste and use that express the needs and norms of contemporary life. The architects Robert Venturi and Denise Scott Brown have analyzed and championed the commonplace for the enrichment of our vision and design vocabulary. The scholar Thomas S. Hines draws on history, sociology, architecture, and a strong sense of the uniquely American experience to show us the true nature of Los Angeles—not as motor city, or nowhere city, but as a place where the native genius of Frank Lloyd Wright, the imported European modernism of Richard Neutra, and the taco huts, pizza palaces, and endless drive-ins of the long, flat boulevards are absorbed and transformed into a rich local culture of unparalleled urban diversity. High and low art, as they have been called, are not polar opposites; they have equal claims to validity. Together, they define our world. Together, they offer the unexpected discoveries and occasional delights in this time of euphemism and pretense that save my sanity and keep me from despair.

I do not deny the needs and tastes well served by those artificial environments that are as American as sliced Wonder bread. Their artificial, wish-fulfilling nature provides a popular alternative to suburban monotony and urban chaos. But the common belief that they represent some kind of immutable, preordained, or universal people's choice, that they have come about through the true exercise of the natural laws of democratic taste and free enterprise, is a fallacy. Contrary to the conventional wisdom, these predictable places are not a pure and spontaneous expression of American culture, as native and all-natural as apple pie. What is being built is the result of the most successful marketing in history; the product is rigidly and restrictively formulaic. Beyond the money machine of the controlled recreational environment of the theme park are the even greater profits to be spun off by the entertainment corporation's ownership of the land around it. The park is the draw; the big payoff comes with the future residential and commercial developments, a fact little-advertised by friendly cartoon characters. These are no Magic Mountains; they are enormous land deals. The business of make-believe, of pretense and playacting, the unreal places we flock to—the theming of America—is one of this country's mammoth real estate investment opportunities. Profit, not planning or, even remotely, public interest, is the generator. If you believe, as I do, that certain environmental entitlements that include social, urban, and aesthetic factors do not figure in these marketing formulas, then the process and the product can be seen as less than inevitable or benign. Nor is it written or engraved or set in concrete that we need to settle for the mediocre and standardized because there are those who like it that way.

I leave to others the higher realms of philosophical definition of the real; my approach is subjective and empirical, based on long acquaintance with the built world and an admitted love of the marvelous mixed heritage and styles that almost four centuries of American life have left upon the land. There are reasons why we so easily support the artificial, the unreal, the substitute, and I have tried to show some of them as well. The idea of authenticity has an interesting history. Miles Orvell has written that the shift from a nineteenth-century culture of imitation and illusion to a twentieth-century culture of authenticity, with its strong underlying moral imperative, was a defining principle of modernism. The desire to reestablish the validity of "the real thing" over the mass-produced replicas and reproductions of Victorian taste fueled an aesthetic that emphasized original artifacts and values. There was no neat break, however, no universal conversion, no rush to embrace a higher truth. The culture of imitation has survived as a major part of the twentieth-century mainstream—Orvell's culture of the factitious. "We have a hunger for something like authenticity," Orvell writes, "but we are easily satisfied by an ersatz facsimile."[2] Today the relationship between the authentic and the factitious is fascinating and increasingly murky.

What interests me as an architectural and urban historian is the transformation of history into fantasy, of the environment into entertainment. What concerns me as a critic is how that affects our attitudes toward the reality of the past, with its remarkable messages of survival and continuity, and the reality of the present, with its equally revealing messages about who and what we are. It is my attachment to the real thing that has made me write this book.

ADA LOUISE HUXTABLE
New York, July 1996

2 MILES ORVELL, *The Real Thing: Imitation and Authenticity in American Culture, 1880–1940* (Chapel Hill: University of North Carolina Press, 1989), xxiii.

Acknowledgments

I am grateful to the American Academy of Arts and Letters for allowing me to express a first version of these thoughts about the unreal America in the Blashfield address delivered on the occasion of the academy ceremonial in May 1991, and to the *New York Review of Books* for printing a revision of the talk (December 3, 1992) and a section on the new architecture (April 6, 1995).

I am particularly grateful to the Graham Foundation for Advanced Studies in the Fine Arts, in Chicago, and to Furthermore, the J. M. Kaplan Fund Publication Program, for generous grants without which this book would not have been possible.

I also wish to express appreciation to Massimo Vignelli for the book's sympathetic and elegant design, which adds so much to its meaning and message; to Joel Honig, for his invaluable assistance in the preparation of the book; and to the architects who patiently and generously provided material for my use. My thanks to Edward O. Nilsson for enthusiasm and assistance that included essential and unorthodox photography, some of which was provided by Caroline Kane of the New York City Landmarks Preservation Commission, and by Laura T. George; and to Peter Nilsson, for making me computer literate. Grace Farrell, my editor at The New Press, and Hall Smyth, art director, provided essential encouragement and expertise.

Introduction

Philosophers have been wrestling with the concept of reality since the beginning of intellectual time. My concern is far less Olympian: it is limited to the physical reality of the world we build, and how what we choose to build affects our lives. We are what we build; stone and steel do not lie; this is real history, about real people and places, at every scale and in every conceivable style. Give or take demolition and natural disasters, architecture is the most immediate, expressive, and lasting art to ever record the human condition.

But there has been a radical change in the way we perceive and understand this world that we have made in our own image, as we move away from its revealing reality in favor of fantasy and invented environments. The cumulative truths of place and past hold few charms, and less interest, for those who prefer to seek entertainment and escape from the disturbing or humdrum aspects of urban and suburban life. The noble concept of the City Beautiful has fallen before the harsh reality of the ghetto, making monuments look absurd. But today's city is more than failed sociology measured against past grandeur; a troubled organism in constant evolution, it is still the repository of the richest record imaginable, available to anyone who looks. There is so much that is so interesting, strange, surprising, and beautiful, so fully alive with meaning, in our cities, now measured in centuries, where unsuspected treasures still guard secret lives. We pay homage to landmarks but are cavalier about their context. The artificial environments we flock to in preference are one-dimensional con games by contrast, their attractions and satisfactions limited, illusory, and equally out for the money.

The change in the way in which we see the world around us—or, rather, don't see it—has had a profound effect on our attitudes toward it. Many basic assumptions about the relationships of art and life that have informed the decision-making and creative process by which places are brought into being are no longer valued or understood. The inherited and inherent principles of the interaction of building and society are either actively ignored or deliberately overturned. Environment is artifice and amusement; it is the theme park with an enormously profitable real estate bottom line and a stunning record as this country's biggest growth industry. Build an "enclave" and you have history; build a multiplex and mall and you have the future. Build a replica of New York in Las Vegas as a skyscraper casino with Coney Island rides and you have a crowd-pleaser without the risk of a trip to the Big Apple. For greater authenticity and more thrills, of course, you could stage hourly simulations of drive-by shootings. (Mock shoot-outs are already a part of the West's tourist-oriented restored ghost towns. Macabre? No more so than a failed proposal by German investors to re-create the Berlin Wall as a theme park in Florida.) Fun City was never like this. Simulation has a logic and special attraction for those who like their jungles plastic and their heroes animatronic, and those who do are legion. Place has no history or validity of its own.

I am convinced that it is this preference for the ersatz experience with its "soft" architecture that has contributed substantially to a great divide, and almost insuperable barrier, between the public's acceptance and understanding of the architecture of our own day and the synthetics that so often usurp its place. With both patrons and public weighing in for the fast fake, serious architecture is having particularly heavy going. Sidelined, trivialized, reduced to a decorative art or a developer's gimmick, characterized by a pastiche of borrowed styles and shaky, subjective references, it is increasingly detached from the problems and processes through which contemporary life and creative necessity are actively engaged. This is a dubious replacement for the rigorous and elegant synthesis of structure, art, utility, and symbolism that has always defined and enriched the building art and made it central to any civilized society.

The expression of these concerns does not mean that this is to be another of those doomsday scripts or tiresome jeremiads against today's art and culture. I write not out of anger or denial, or as a lament for the past, with the converted who preach the gospel according the Prince Charles, that architecture needs to be purged of the twentieth century and put back on a classical course to regain some illusory legitimacy and set everything right. I cannot think of anything more ludicrous than the idea that modernism somehow got off the track and was a monstrous mistake that should simply be canceled out. Revolutions in life and technology can never be reversed. All art is deeply rooted in the reality of its own present. To remain uninvolved with one's own day is to deny all that is vital and alive and intrinsic to a legitimate late-twentieth-century art and style. But modernism also taught us that we ignore history at our peril. And it is the process of change that links the present and the past in a fierce and wonderful embrace of relevance and revelation.

If what we are getting is what we want, there is no argument. But if what we are getting is what we are being given, out of shrewd self-interest, simple greed, masterful marketing, and the art of the deal—arguably the greatest American art of all—then we are being had. The redundant clones of the entrepreneurial environment sell short the popular culture that its promoters and proponents claim to elevate and embrace. For many, unknowing and uncaring, there is no loss involved. For others, the taste for pop exploitation represents a chic superrealism with a cutting-edge cachet, a perversely trendy avant-garde. But there is something fundamentally disquieting when the knowledgeable join the naive in trashing the richer reality. It is time to question fashionable attitudes and the conventional wisdom about what we value and the way we build. Architecture as packaging or playacting, as disengagement from reality, is a notion whose time, alas, seems to have come.

THE UNREAL AMERICA

Never Was

previous page: History as Photo Op: the Queen Mother at Colonial Williamsburg. *Courtesy of Colonial Williamsburg.*

left: History as Stage Set: Duke of Gloucester Street, Colonial Williamsburg. *Courtesy of Colonial Williamsburg.*

I do not know just when we lost our sense of reality or interest in it, but at some point it was decided that reality was not the only option; that it was possible, permissible, and even desirable to improve on it; that one could substitute a more agreeable product. It followed that reality was, first, mutable and then expendable; its substance was abdicated for what could be revised and manipulated. Downgrading the evidence of the built world—its cities and its structures—has profoundly affected architecture and urbanism. One would think that these hard physical facts would present a reality so absolute, so irrefutable, that it would be difficult to distort, deny, or trivialize it. These places that are the containers of life and experience—the mother lode of societies and cultures—have always provided an amazing account of the human condition in all of its uncommon, unpredictable, and unexpected diversity. The built record, which holds most of the lessons of art and history, is there for anyone to see; but, increasingly, we have not wanted to see it. Or we have preferred to pretty it up, to reconfigure it for other purposes. Denial has spread like a virus, invading, infecting, and changing architectural and urban standards in the most basic sense.

The replacement of reality with selective fantasy is a phenomenon of that most successful and staggeringly profitable American phenomenon, the reinvention of the environment as themed entertainment. The definition of "place" as a chosen image probably started in a serious way in the late 1920s at Colonial Williamsburg, predating and paving the way for the new world order of Walt Disney Enterprises. Certainly it was in the restoration of Colonial Williamsburg that the studious fudging of facts received its scholarly imprimatur, and that history and place as themed artifact hit the big time. Williamsburg is seen by the cognoscenti as a kind of period piece now, its shortsightedness a product of the limitations of the early preservation movement. Within a conscientious range of those deliberately and artfully set limitations, a careful construct was created: a place where one could learn a little romanticized history, confuse the real and unreal, and have—then and now—a very nice time. Knowledge, techniques, and standards have become increasingly sophisticated in the intervening years, and there have been escalating efforts to keep up. But it is the Williamsburg image and example as originally conceived that has spread and multiplied, that continues to be universally admired and emulated.

Restoration is a difficult and unclear procedure at best; unreality is built into the process, which requires a highly subjective kind of cosmetic surgery that balances life and death. At Williamsburg, there was instant amputation with the conceit of a "cutoff date" for the restoration—in this case, 1770, an arbitrary determination of when, and for what purpose, a place should be frozen in time. After the cutoff date had been chosen, the next step for the undertaking has been to "restore it back"; both euphemisms are official preservationese. "Restoring back" means re-creating a place as someone thinks it was—or would like it to have been—at a certain chosen moment, eliminating everything else that was not there at the time. This usually means moving or destroying a good deal of subsequent architectural history—exactly the stuff of which real history and art are made. Fashions in preservation and appalling good taste are part of the mix. In an act of stunning illogic and innocent hubris, a consortium of preservation architects and historical soothsayers plays God, with assists from the spirits of Emily Post and Elsie de Wolfe.

As practiced in this country, these linguistic and conceptual crimes against art and history have achieved complete acceptance and respectability. They have become established elements of popular culture. They have also given a license to destroy. Approximately 730 buildings were removed at Williamsburg; 81 were renovated and 413 were rebuilt on the original sites.[1] Everything later than the chosen time frame had to disappear. So much for reality. And so much for the messy, instructive, invaluable, and irretrievable revelations that are part of the serendipitous record of urban settlements. In Williamsburg, prerestoration photographs showed a range of post-Colonial buildings of valid later styles. They were real, of course, but they were inappropriate to the cutoff date, and so they were bulldozed or removed. This becomes a slippery game. The next step replaces the "wrong" buildings with the "right" buildings, moved, in turn, from somewhere else. To complete the stage set, major buildings that no longer existed are reconstructed—at Williamsburg, the Capitol. That decision involved some Alice in Wonderland architectural hairsplitting about whether to reproduce the first or second version of the building, neither of which had been there for quite some time. (The second burned in 1832.) Much was made of the available documentary evidence, which, it has turned out, was fraught with interpretive booby traps; we know now that bitter debate accompanied questionable conclusions.

When it comes to furnishing and equipping these re-created settings, the dreams and ambitions of curators take over, and collections of awesome and improbable museum quality are assembled. Occasionally there is the coup of a piece of furniture or an object returned to its original home. Much that is only tenuously connected to what might have been is rationalized by the phrase "of the period." Elegant and elaborate curtains and upholstery from fabric manufacturers known for historic reproductions inevitably follow, as day follows night, inspiring upscale decorator lines. Details of rebuilt or restored structures are copied from the more splendid examples, locally or abroad, or from pattern books— always "of the period." At this point, reason disintegrates; carriages and costumes and all the appurtenances of make-believe take over— in the interest of an ersatz reality, of course, as well as of the tourist trade. (I am still bemused by a television series, purportedly on architecture, in which the postmodernist architects Leon Krier and Robert A. M. Stern, riding in one of those carriages, blithely praised the spurious and the silly at Williamsburg. This philosophical joyride led to their enthusiastic endorsement, once all rational standards were abandoned, of a vaguely Williamsburged suburban shopping center of depressingly bottomless banality as a really neat idea.)

The blend of new and old, real and fake, original and copy, even in the best of these restorations, defies separation or analysis; they are all, in the beginning and the end, an artificial invention that is supposed to tell us, truly, what our art and history were like. But at the same time that they supposedly teach something to those who might otherwise remain innocent of history, they devalue what they teach; the intrinsic qualities of the real are transformed and falsified by an experience that is itself the ultimate unreality.

In his brilliant and energetic pursuit of this curiously American phenomenon of glorifying the unreal over the real, Umberto Eco observes that for a reconstruction to be credible "it must be absolutely iconic, a perfect likeness, a 'real' copy of the reality being presented."[2] Writing with as insightful and revealing an eye on a people and their practices as de Tocqueville's observations on democracy, he notes that "the American imagination demands the

[1] MARCUS WHIFFEN, *The Public Buildings of Williamsburg* (Williamsburg, Va.: Colonial Williamsburg, Inc., 1958), v.

[2] UMBERTO ECO, *Travels in Hyper Reality*. William Weaver, trans. (New York: Harcourt, Brace Jovanovich, 1986).

real thing, and to attain it, must fabricate the absolute fake…for historical information to be absorbed, it has to assume the aspect of a reincarnation…the 'completely real' becomes the 'completely fake'…absolute unreality is offered as real presence." It follows that the restoration must be more real, or better than real, superior to any natural survivor. And, of course, the housekeeping will be immensely better, making it all more acceptable and inviting.

A visit to these places can be extremely pleasant if one suspends all discomfort about accuracy and mixed messages. The average tourist is routinely lulled into believing that this is the way it was—tidied up a little, naturally, with a bit of slippage in the story being told for a more attractive product, and with a few good restaurants added, preferably with local historical cuisine. The ladies in hoopskirts, who have exchanged their 1930s saddle shoes for Reeboks under their petticoats, tell you that this is so. Only someone as churlish as I, knowing and caring too much, could be consistently put off by the experience. At one point (I confess to being agent provocateur in my journalist role at the *New York Times*) there was some effort to indicate what had actually survived in situ at Williamsburg, if not exactly what had been done to it, and to identify what were increasingly called "authentic reproductions," a term that has filled an unreal need where none existed before.

My loathing of the term "authentic reproduction" goes deep; these are the con words of American culture. The use and influence of the phrase are universal, cutting across almost all cultural levels. I cannot think of a more mischievous, dangerous, anomalous, and shoddy perversion of language and meaning. A perfect contradiction in terms, it makes no sense at all; but what particularly offends is its smug falseness, its dissembling, genteel pretentiousness. Authentic is the real thing, and a reproduction, by definition, is not; a copy is still a copy, no matter how skilled or earnest its intentions. To equate a replica with the genuine artifact is the height of sophistry; it cheapens and renders meaningless its true age and provenance. To imply equal value is to deny the act of creation within its own time frame, to cancel out the generative forces of its cultural context. What is missing is the original mind, hand, material, and eye. The kindest thing you can say is that an authentic reproduction is a genuine oxymoron.

"Authentic reproduction" has entered the language as a total up-ending of values and a great moneymaker for historic restorations, museums, and assorted coattail enterprises. What interests me is how far this easy confusion of fact and fantasy has come, and how insidiously it has corrupted the way we think. Whether or not we relegate the premises of Williamsburg to the mists of preservation time, its popularity and progeny have taught us to subvert reality on a grand scale, to prefer—and believe in—the sanitized and selective version of the past. This has led to the denial of the diversity and eloquence of change and continuity, and to the devaluation of those deposits of history and humanity that make our cities vehicles of a special kind of art and experience without parallel or peer. Of course, we like our memories better all cleaned up. The gritty and sometimes unlovely accumulations that characterize cities are the best and worst of what we have produced; they exert a fascination that no neatly edited version can inspire. I have enormous respect and affection for this record; it never ceases to reward and intrigue me. I have never stopped learning from it or marveling at its surprises. From the magnificence representing the highest human aspirations to the decayed dreams of serious social failure, it has the wonder and distinction and example of being the real thing. I have spent much time exploring those imperfect, glorious to grungy accumulations of urban experience, with the unexpected revelations of value and meaning so richly embedded in everything from high art to the art of the commonplace. The variety of ordinary styles and patterns in a few city blocks offers more information and pleasure than the sterile clichés of any artificial substitute. To edit life, to sanitize the substance of history, is to risk losing the art, actuality, and meaning of the real past and its intrinsic artifacts.

These preservation "enclaves" are frequently an assortment of developer-dispossessed fragments given a new "olde" name after having been moved from places where they were inconveniently interfering with profitable new construction. When reality does occasionally rear its ambiguous head in the curious collection of castoffs, the whole business collapses. Although some historians have always suspected that Williamsburg might be too good to be true, serious revisionism is relatively recent. A second, more "scientific" look at the evidence has resulted in a drastic revision of the long-revered "correct" paint colors, from discreetly muted and infinitely salable Williamsburg blues and greens to much gaudier hues. In the further interest of "authenticity," management introduced some pigs to roam the too tidy streets, although their role has been changed from scavengers of garbage to picturesque props. (The addition of livestock in these so-called authentic restorations has

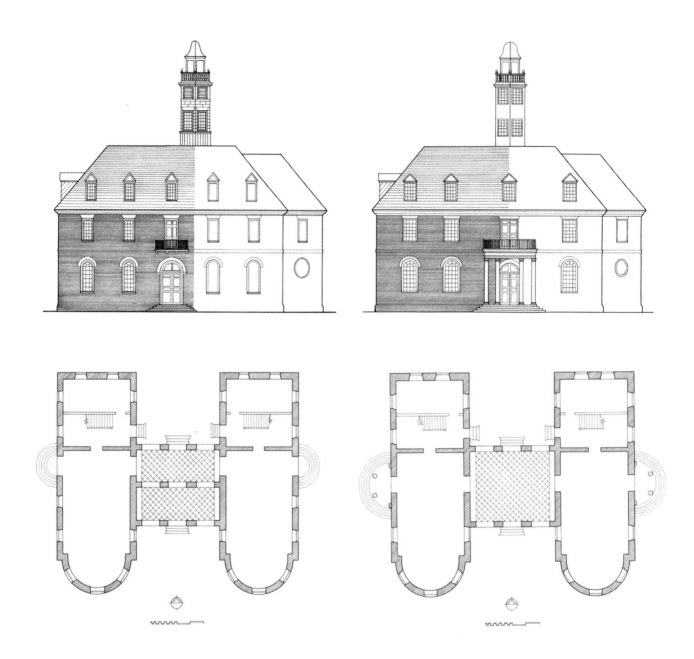

The Capitol at Colonial Williamsburg, reconstructed in 1932-33 by using foundation remains and pictorial references, elevation and plan, *right,* is a building of classical symmetry. Fifty years later, a new study of the same sources by Carl R. Lounsbury indicated a corrected interpretation with an off-center facade and layout, elevation and plan, *left. Drawings courtesy of Carl R. Lounsbury and the Colonial Williamsburg Foundation.*

brought along another anomaly—"breeding back" for more "authentic" animals.) These things snowball into a kind of circular lunacy. Historians are aware of the dilemma, and there is a lot of scholarly soul-searching going on in Williamsburg and other places about how to increase the authenticity of the imitation. Younger historians have even committed the heresy of claiming that the Williamsburg Capitol is not that authentic at all.

The rebuilders of the reconstructed Capitol have now been accused of redesigning it. It takes just about a half century for the cycles of taste and style to turn, for one revelation to be replaced by another. More recent scholarship[3] has suggested that the original documents and foundation remains were misread in the 1930s. Taught to think in terms of the formal classical symmetry of their Beaux Arts training, the reconstruction architects could not believe, or accept, that the building's axis could have been off-center. The entrance contradicts the evidence of the foundation and is probably in the wrong place. Other spatial relationships are also questionable.

Beyond virtually unavoidable technical errors, authentic reproductions will always be false. Few historical documents are immune to interpretation. Such undertakings are processed through the eyes and minds of subsequent generations. Still, this kind of reconstruction has taken on an aura of natural, or national, correctness. Foreign dignitaries are welcomed at Williamsburg by the State Department and provided with photo ops in carriages. Because the best documents and the most astute detective work are rarely definitive, new directors and attitudes and the passage of time lead to "revisions," each touted as more authentic than the last. In fact, the differing interpretive visions and their mutations are as interesting for what they teach us about changing tastes and viewpoints as for their exposure of the limited, wishful, and often demonstrably false first readings of the experts. To track the life of a restoration is to learn a great deal about art, history, and reality.

Then what are we to do about the past? Sacrifice it to the conventional wisdom of amiable evasion and commercial viability? Bow to the inevitability of destruction and loss? Continue to exploit and distort it, turning it into a crude caricature and crowd-pleaser while

3 CARL R. LOUNSBURY, "Beaux-Arts Ideals and Colonial Reality: The Reconstruction of Williamsburg's Capitol, 1928-1934" *Journal of the Society of Architectural Historians*, December 1990, 373–389.

pointing piously to what we have "saved?" Obviously, we will continue to follow that course because we do it so well. More glossy coffee-table books will display glorious, full-color, oversize photographs of our "successes." This face-saving, artifact-saving formula has become enormously popular and profitable, whatever its fictions or manipulative distortions. These historic restorations and re-creations are, however, becoming increasingly expensive to maintain, with growing fund-raising problems. And some of us will be increasingly conflicted about the results.

In fact, we have learned a great deal since the Williamsburg model. We understand much more about the past and its complex relationships with the present. At best, preservation is a necessary but ambiguous effort; there is nothing tidy about it. We know that preservation is a complex and subtle component of larger urban and environmental issues. We have come to understand the past as both place and process, to see the architectural aesthetic in its social and cultural context. The movement has come a long way, from the primitive nostalgia of "George Washington slept here" to the sophisticated creation of historic districts as part of municipal policy and law. But its most popular and successful by-product is the high-class historical theme park and its more commercial clones.

Fortunately, there has also been increasing recognition of those surviving modest streets and buildings, spontaneous accretions of character and history, that capture and keep the past as part of the present. Their surprising stylistic range has made them difficult to declare as protected districts, and even more difficult to deal with. These anonymous urban survivals are essentially unmanageable in academic or aesthetic terms, since individual buildings may lack "landmark" status or a scholarly seal of approval; they do not fit into the established "great building" or "historic house" mold. They have tended to fall like dominoes under developer attack and in courts of law, until cumulative preservation decisions strengthened their legal claims. Unfortunately, the idea of the isolated landmark divorced from its setting is surprisingly tenacious. It underlies the criteria of some early preservation statutes, which were often based on the dramatic rescue of a single threatened structure; it is a standard that still tends to be most persuasive with preservation boards and commissions. At best, these areas present a Hobson's choice: unrestrained interventions shatter their fragile fabric; restrictive regulations take the life out of them. In either case, a definitive and inevitable transformation results.

Rows of eighteenth- and nineteenth-century buildings, accidental survivors of relentless rebuilding in Lower Manhattan, keep the past as part of the present by adapting continuously and unself-consciously to new needs. *Photos, Joel Honig and A. L. Huxtable.*

The natural accretions of time and taste add up to the lively diversity of New York's Nassau Street.

The designation of such areas as landmark districts starts a process of homogenization, an economic, cultural, and physical upgrading in which everything is made to resemble what it might have once been —only better. The act of preservation turns what has been "saved" into something else, at the same time that the improvements provide the economic base that "saves" it. This is classic Catch-22. Sooner or later, image and function are defined and fixed in an artificial formula that combines sentiment, fashion, and tourist appeal. Still, it is hard to be ungrateful when the alternative is destruction or degenerative decay of the historic heart of the city. The dilemma has no easy answers; it allows no glib judgments. In a perceptive essay, the Swiss urban historian André Corboz has posed the essential and inescapable question: will there be nothing in the historic centers of America or Europe, he asks, between "a tourism that denatures them and a squalor that degrades them?"[4]

I am not arguing for an end to preservation; I have fought too long and too hard for heritage consciousness and preservation legislation, for stylistic survival, for the recognition of the beauty and necessity of older and undervalued buildings. The cherishing of the aesthetic and urban achievements of the past is critical to the quality of our environment and our lives. To lose history is to lose place, identity, and meaning. But continuity can be achieved only if the past is integrated into the contemporary context in a way that works and matters. Our awareness and appreciation of historic buildings and neighborhoods must be coupled with a sensitivity to and desire for their continued relevance and use, for their "connectedness," for the way they bridge the years and the continuum of social, cultural, urban, and architectural history. It is their recycling and adaptation that will keep them as a living part of today's cities and communities. Their uses may be unconventional; they may even become marginal; they may offer a casual palimpsest rather than textbook history; they will certainly be impure rather than pure—if there is really anything admirable about that kind of pedantic reduction to irrelevance.

Is it possible to suggest the unthinkable: that "historic preservation," like "authentic reproduction," is often an illusory reality, a contradiction in terms, that its success contains the paradox of

4 ANDRÉ CORBOZ, *Looking for a City in America: Down These Mean Streets a Man Must Go...* Angel's Flight, Occasional Papers from Los Angeles. (Santa Monica: Getty Center for the History of Art and the Humanities, 1992) First published as "Non-City Revisited" in *La Ville Inquiète*. (Paris: Editions Gallimard, 1987). p. 57

failure? Unlike the complete sham of "authentic reproduction," the idea of historic preservation starts with authentic material; the process changes authenticity into artificiality. If authentic reproduction is a conceptual and linguistic fallacy, historic preservation is more properly a semantic trap. Its definitions and desires are set by the seductions of what survives—those rare, real, evanescent, and evocative pieces of the past that are ultimately betrayed or excised by the unreality of the restoration.

To express profound unease or to pose this question—when so many dedicated professionals struggle with the enormous task of dealing with complex regulations, uncertain finances, and growing commercial competition while they try to keep what they know should not be lost—is to be considered remote and unsympathetic. One is perceived as an enemy of the cause. I do not deny the need for the past, or the legitimacy and necessity of the movement that carries the preservation name, or the tragedy of the lost past when the destruction is brutal and willful. But I believe we can no longer evade the reality of what we have achieved by expedient distortion or deliberate simulacrum, in forms to suit transient tastes and economic imperatives. In fact, to raise these issues at all, one must love the past very much.

History is quicksilver that runs at the touch; it refers to events that derived their life, breath, color, and meaning from some elusive shaping moment in the irretrievable past. It is both charged and changed by the prism of passing time. The essential, defining clues of a particular moment may not even survive. By its very definition, history is something that is gone forever. Do the passage of time and the irreversible effects of that inexorable process, seen through our shifting, conditioned responses, make preservation an erudite, often misleading game, with artificially embalmed remains and suspiciously elegant artifacts? Does it not follow that inventions and simulacra, of things that existed and things that did not, will be given equal value and credibility? Is it tempting to value them more than the shabby, incomplete survivals? Must one always exorcise the ghosts for costumed extras?

The questions are rhetorical; this has, in fact, already happened. We acknowledge our need for the signs and signifiers of time and place by reference and association, but we insist that those signs and signifiers are replicable. Both Eco and Jean Baudrillard have pointed out that the copy is not only preferred, it is now taken as the thing itself. The past must have immediate, corporeal presence. "Our entire linear and accumulative culture would collapse if we could not stockpile the past in plain view," Baudrillard has observed.[5] In this reading, the improved re-creation is valued over the flawed original or shabby survival; it is considered more iconic, representative, ideal, and congenial. For most, it has become the reality.

What the perfect fake or impeccable restoration lacks are the hallmarks of time and place. They deny imperfections, alterations, and acccomodations; they wipe out all the incidents of life and change. The worn stone, the chafed corner, the threshold low and uneven from many feet, the marks on walls and windows that carry the presence and message of remembered hands and eyes—all of those accumulated, accidental, suggestive, and genuine imprints that imbue the artifact with its history and continuity, that have stayed with it in its conditioning passage through time—are absent or erased. There is nothing left of the journey from there to here, nothing that palpably joins the past to the present, that makes direct physical and emotional contact with the viewer, the bittersweet link with those who have been there before. What are gone are the cumulative clues, the patina of age and use, the sense of "others"—that essential, irreplaceable quality that Stephen Greenblatt has so insightfully called "resonance."[6] It is this resonance that gives an object "the power…to reach out beyond its formal boundaries to a larger world, to invoke in the viewer the complex, dynamic cultural forces from which it has emerged." Significantly, it is precisely this central, intrinsic quality that has been eliminated from the reproduction, that no longer exists in the restoration. These objects and places simply do not resonate. They are mute. They are hollow history.

The more conscientious or careful the restoration, the larger the doubts and discomforts likely to be raised. In awarding a prize to the restoration of Ellis Island, a jury coupled praise with troubling questions: "Does this building in its polished and gleaming freshness correctly convey the sense of history this hallowed place should engender?" the citation asked. Answering the pointed

5 JEAN BAUDRILLARD, *Simulations*. Paul Foss, Paul Patton, and Philip Beitchman, trans. (New York: Semiotext(e), 1983), p. 19.

6 STEPHEN GREENBLATT, "Resonance and Wonder," *Bulletin of the American Academy of Arts and Sciences* (January 1990): 11-34.

Abandoned chairs in Ellis Island's empty and decaying rooms could speak of transition and displacement with more eloquence than artful museum arrangement of speciman baggage and computer-generated information displays in the same space today. In the completed restoration, all the ghosts are gone. *Prerestoration 1954 photographs by Shirley Burden, courtesy of the Museum of the City of New York. Restored baggage room courtesy of the architects, Beyer Blinder Belle.*

query with what can only be called a sincere waffle, the text concluded that "although the very newness of the result may seem at odds with the project's commitment to history, it is so skillfully executed and thoughtfully conceived, that [it] deserves the highest commendation."[7] A not inconsiderable factor was that the historic gateway for America's immigrants in New York's harbor had been saved for future generations. Still, A for effort begs serious misgivings. A skilled and scrupulous conversion to a memorial and museum has exorcised all ghosts. Memories have been edited. The shabby, littered halls and abandoned, scattered chairs that still retain the presence of those who came and went, who waited to be processed, received, or rejected, the transience, crowding and anxiety, the sense of endings and beginnings, the untidiness and uncertainties of the historical process, have been reduced to an artfully arranged display of old luggage. What it was like exists only in a remarkable set of original 1954 photographs by Shirley Burden, filled with resonance and wonder.

Today's Ellis Island has a completely different style. Tasteful relacement parts and neat modern details, cliché commercial displays of informative push-and-light-up exhibits, handsomely restored Guastavino vaulting in the great hall that seems more attuned to catering than to a cacophony of languages—everything has an earnest educational air and a careful "good design" gloss. Even the much visited wall of names is too precisely metallic, too unimpressive and impersonal in material and scale, underwhelming in its lack of monumentality, grandeur, and suggestion. This is a tidy, mechanical roll call. The place is—simply—something else.

As a privileged visitor allowed to wander through unrestored buildings on the island, I was able to find its poignant identity again. The hospital of endless corridors,[8] lined with miles of broken, continuous window sash and an occasional abandoned bed, was a revolutionary, light-filled building where those with infectious diseases were quarantined. Shadows filtered through trees into the many open courtyards of the remarkable plan where tubercular patients were wheeled for sun and air. The morgue of this early teaching hospital, with its concrete slab and small

7 ALBERT S. BARD AWARD, presented in 1992 by the City Club of New York to outstanding works of architecture and urban design.

8 The hospital is now on the World Monuments Fund list of most endangered buildings for its design and medical innovations.

amphitheater of rising seats above it, summons up a *terribilità* of human pathos and scientific mission. Pigeons fly through corner towers open to the sky, the rubble of roofs and layers of leaves crumbling on the stairs underfoot. Abandonment has its own meaning and message, a direct contact with what once was that disappears with restoration—one of those anomalies with no answer. In the restored main hall, what you see is what you get— and what you get is not what it was.

No one wants to face the possibility that salvation self-destructs when the alternative is loss or ruin; the trade-off is too painfully clear to contemplate. Inevitably, there are some extraordinary mixed signals and some very unsettling messages being sent, as well as a notable reluctance to receive them. A genuine concern for the past does not prevent intellectual, historical, and artistic distortions from taking place. There are stunning ambiguities involved, a familiar state in so many aspects of art and life today. Doubt, double meaning, and ironic side effects have become a kind of leading cultural indicator of our time.

What we find is that we have invented a new past according to a set of criteria designed to satisfy our own current needs and standards. This has always been so, of course; revisionism is part of the historical process. In today's fractured and deeply troubled society the need is for something that comforts, reassures, and entertains—a world where harsh truths can be suspended or forgotten for a benign and soothing, preferably distracting, substitute. The nostalgic simplifications of feel-good, participatory, romanticized history are the popular and profitable answer. To reinforce the myth of more rigorous "interpretation" and accuracy, we use increasingly sophisticated tools of invention and support: the "scientific" research of chemistry, the computer, skilled domestic archaeology, the discipline and discoveries of materials culture. The familiar, formulaic procedure defines the brand of preservation that has become a staple of today's tourism, and it is not incidental that tourism is an increasingly important part of local economies, often the main support of small historic towns that have lost their business base to suburban malls.

Finally, the environmental end-product and the economic bottom line are the same. The unsurprisingly similar "historic whatever" —of varying degrees of convenient invention and scholarly relia- bility, on a well-defined tourist track, market-driven, supported by market research—is a predictable product and a business that have their own rules and circular irony. If something is to be saved, the costs must be paid; if the costs are to be paid, the money must be available; to get the money, the product must sell; to sell, it must appeal; which brings it right back to the market again. The struggle for funds cannot stop. So market-minded, in fact, do some of the most dedicated preservation groups become, through actual need or carefully solicited business advice (or both), that as recently as the early go-go 1980s Colonial Williamsburg was considering the demolition of a neighborhood of perfectly good early-twentieth-century houses, judged expendable under the self-imposed rules of eighteenth-century reference and relevance, for an investment development of town houses of tenuous traditional recall. The idea was protested and dropped, one suspects as much for a weak real estate market as for objections of principle. But preservation, development, and real estate have become a very comfortable ménage à trois, conspicuously in bed together. The savers and the spoilers have joined to give us a conceptual and aesthetic product that ranges from confusion to corruption, characteristic of no other place or time.

The easiest way is to stay with the popular idea of historic preservation as an entertainment and educational package of at least marginal commercial viability. That keeps the problem out of the developers' way and hair. Admittedly, to do anything else is to go a more difficult route. Such efforts are usually due to stubbornly dedicated private leadership working against the grain, with a sympathetic public or private preservation body to overcome infinite procedural obstacles. Unfortunately, the more familiar model carries a near-universal stamp of approval, even as it offers all the wrong lessons and considerable disinformation. The harm it does is to confirm for many that this is the only way to go, that a heritage is being saved by cordoning off, sanitizing, and redefining an artificial piece of the past. Neatness counts.

Because this cop-out is so widely accepted, the real losses are neither acknowledged nor understood, nor ultimately dealt with. Even among those equipped to judge, there is an inability or unwillingness to understand that a battle can be won and lost at the same time. It is hard to be clear-eyed about what these Pyrrhic victories do to the subject under siege; there is an understandable reluctance to face the problem when no easy answers exist. Nor is it the American way to define a dilemma without providing a solution.

By now, of course, vested interests are served through entrenched belief or financial involvement. But I see no reason for righteous rationalization or circuitous justification of the results; there is no real defense for the kind of transformation of the past that is increasingly approaching what Baudrillard has called, in another context, "extermination by museumification."[9]

There are answers, but they require profound changes in philosophy and support. The problems of site-and-use preservation are enormous but not insurmountable. They must be understood in terms of immediate benefit and long-term gain and treated as appropriate public and national priorities. Unfortunately, that kind of preservation has no connection with public policy, which determines both public and private action and expenditure. Public policy in this country, particularly in Republican administrations, is to see expenditures for preservation as in a league with original sin. Other countries treat the national heritage as a national responsibility. The beauty of Paris is no accident; the protection and maintenance of its urban and architectural heritage are a state-funded policy and priority. In the United States, the public sector has no funds for urban investment, least of all for anything that involves appropriate planning and design. Private investment defines quality of life as some up-front luxury trim and a few recreational amenities thrown in by the developer. Public policy militates against anything better; private interests recognize only exploitative and potentially profitable flourishes. When tax credits that encourage reuse of old buildings are proved to work, to the benefit of both people and cities, they are compromised or repealed, while perennially generous real estate incentives are promoted that favor destruction and, often, shoddy new construction. When a rare program of vision is passed, developers usually find ingenious ways to profitably subvert the objectives, while government builds leaden bureaucracies that do the same thing.

Just after World War II, the Italians demonstrated an extraordinary sensibility to the problems and solutions of rebuilding in a historic context. Modern interventions were skillfully and elegantly inserted into historic cities without copying or second-guessing the past; Italian architects designed and carried out their work in a way that beautifully defined their own creative moment through tacit differences between old and new in style and use, while establishing

9 BAUDRILLARD, Ibid., 20–21.

Historic architecture enhances new uses in Boston's Old City Hall, *top,* remodeled for offices and restaurants, and New York's Astor Library, bottom, now in its third incarnation as the New York Shakespeare Festival and Public Theater, after it had been abandoned by the Hebrew Immigrant Aid Society.

a rich and explicit continuity of urban history and form. This method, marvelously successful in older European cities, was subsequently grossly misunderstood and misapplied, particularly in the United States and Great Britain, where incongruity passed as comity at the height of the modern movement. Maybe what was lacking in those brutal or banal juxtapositions was the history-steeped, fine Italian eye and hand. With few exceptions, most architects preferred to demolish anything old for anything new.

Today, an inevitable backlash against modernism's aggressive anti-historicism has rejected this approach for an emphasis on "period" infill of "matching" styles, a safe and sterile response that begs many questions about art and history and genuine contextualism. "The profession of urban design is almost wholly preoccupied with reproduction, with the creation of urbane disguises," writes the critic Michael Sorkin.[10] There may be times and places where this method is the appropriate course, but the circumstances are special and few. The most notorious example of this blinkered vision is probably the area around St. Paul's in London, a precinct so atrociously reconstructed after World War II in a flabby modernism of total architectural and urban vacuity and irrelevance that an unavoidable backlash—aided by the ever vigilant Prince Charles—has foreclosed any rebuilding possibilities except as a pastiche of the past. In Washington, D.C., the art of historical camouflage is being given a special twist: the nation's capital is being Disneyfied with whole streets of carefully amputated eighteenth- and nineteenth-century facades, cunningly retained and prettily restored as literal false fronts for outsize new buildings erected directly behind them. These "preserved" streetscapes look as if they have been wheeled in, like stage flats; one half expects appropriately costumed performers to jump out and sing. Or at least walk around, shake hands, and pose for pictures with the tourists, à la Mickey and Goofy. Surely a dubious-achievement award should go to this insane compromise that succeeds in making fakes out of something real.

My objective in this long critique is not to prove anything right or wrong, good or bad; we are a country much too fond of analyses and solutions in black and white. I am dedicated to the continuity of that vulnerable heritage that defines us and adds immeasurably to our quality of life. To make that possible, we need honest evalua-

---

10 Michael Sorkin, ed., *Variations on a Theme Park: The New American City and the End of Public Space* (New York: Hill and Wang, 1992), xiv.

tions of what matters and why; such anonymous, hard-to-label survivals fail to pass outmoded definitions or fit rigidly preestablished criteria. We need to recognize and admit that the preservation movement has had both resounding successes and mixed and dubious results, that we need a reevaluation of objectives and methods on both the public and private fronts. I might even dare to hope for some recognition of the advantages of ambiguity and its rewarding dual readings of past and present, even to suggest that we might find ways to incorporate that rich palimpsest of experience and aesthetics into the contemporary urban and human condition. This cannot happen while we insist that, intellectually and morally, the distinctions be kept clear between one thing and another, past and present, old and new, with the help of some scholarly or popular fudging; we prefer hypocrisy to loose ends.

I am devoted to the principle that every age produces its greatest buildings in its own image. I believe that the art and act of contemporary design must be rooted in, and cannot avoid, the conditions and references of its own time. Ultimately, it is the addition and absorption of this continuous record of changing art, technology, ideas, and uses that make cities unique repositories of the whole range of human endeavor. Within this understanding and context, there is a preservation principle that can, and should, apply. There are viable criteria: the manner in which the historical setting accomodates change, the degree to which style and identity support authentic functions, and the frequency with which destruction is avoided by legitimate continuity through an appropriate role in contemporary life and use. All this determines whether, and how, and in what manner, we keep our heritage—and the meaning and worth and success of the effort. The past lives only as part of the present. The results will never be perfect, but they will be real.

America the Faux

It has been a very short distance down the yellow brick road of fantasy from Williamsburg to Disneyland. Both are quintessentially American inventions. Both deal in stunningly doctored reality. What they have in common is their suspension of disbelief, the expertise of their illusion, and the espousal of a skillfully edited, engineered, and marketed version of a chosen place or theme. In Disneyparks, the inaccessible and exotic can be enjoyed conveniently, comfortably, and interchangeably; Swiss and Polynesian villages coexist at friendly scale in close proximity. More people have experienced Disney's fantasy environments than have visited the places that have inspired them; the clean and cozy, abbreviated and adulterated versions of the Vieux Carré or Garden District of New Orleans, divested of the distractions of dirt, crime, and ethnic diversity, are preferred to the city itself. Curiously, in this inversion of reality, some of the most romantically remote places, no longer inaccessible, have become crowded and polluted versions of the original ideal.

The miniaturized Matterhorn of Disneyland is a California landmark, seen from the freeway. Now a Disney export, it can be seen again from the highway outside Tokyo. There is no cynicism in the Disney creation of Main Street, U.S.A., even as Main Streets die across the country; there is simply no connection made between the two. Fantasy and selectively re-created reality have become an undifferentiated whole, in which the change of function to evocative entertainment cancels out the meaning and value of history and form. There is no longer an attachment to actuality. The appropriated is validated over the source.

The rejection of reality, or unwillingness to come to grips with it in favor of something easier and pleasanter, is not a new American phenomenon. There is a legitimate tradition here, of sorts; so much of this country has been created out of wishful thinking and whole cloth. So much has been invented by those who never knew the original or knew it only secondhand, or had a remarkable instinct for the exploitation and transformation of precedents to serve some new and unrelated purpose or context. The platting of gridded new towns on vast, blank tracts of land for a westward-moving population was both an act of necessity and an exercise in unparalleled bravura. The 1811 plan that ruled off Manhattan Island into uniform, salable lots ran the grid over hills, valleys, and farms, turning nature into a historic real estate opportunity. The Hispano-Moresque resorts in Florida, with imported palm trees and imitation boiserie that were devised after World War I by Addison Mizner for the Pullman-car commuting superrich, were interventions of will and imagination combined with a shrewd instinct for timely capitalization. (It was not uncommon for his clients to find identical cracks and stress marks in their instantly aged château paneling.) All have left a legacy of fantasy that shaped the look of the land and the lives of their users.

Today that tabula rasa heritage and attitude continue in real estate developments that cannibalize bits and pieces of history, and in planned communities using precedents that recall earlier vernacular styles and older, gentler times. New towns like Seaside, Florida, and Kentlands, Maryland, designed by Andres M. Duany and Elizabeth Plater-Zyberk, are exploding across the landscape; they are the expert prototypes for neotraditional residential developments based on a past ideal of community that has become part of the mythology of the American dream. Duany–Plater-Zyberk's new towns are skillful demonstrations of how well this idealized image can be re-created by able and believing architects; the results, easy to like, are a conscientious contradiction in terms. By reducing the definition of community to a romantic social aesthetic emphasizing front porches, historic styles, and walking distance to stores and schools as an answer to suburban sprawl— that post–World War II domestic American dream that has fallen out of favor as suburban problems have multiplied—they have avoided the questions of urbanization to become part of the problem. Only now are the proponents of a nostalgic regionalism beginning to focus on the revitalization of older communities in the inner city.

Like so much that has gone before, these towns are places from scratch, executed with a scholarly knowledge of architectural styles and a sophisticated understanding of the craving for the kind of neighborhood community that disappeared with an extinct way of life. Herbert Muschamp points out that the modernists and neotraditionalists are alike in their reliance "on esthetic solutions to the social problems created by urban sprawl." Also like the modernists, who "created machine-age images of 'rational' cities that, when actually built, often functioned miserably," these appealing and simplistically pretty towns ignore the history and messages of reality for an idealized small-town reality. Iconic evocations of intimacy and stability, they have a strong appeal for a mobile, family-fragmented society. "Architecture for the

Inventing places continues today in new towns by Andres M. Duany and Elizabeth Plater-Zyberk, where nostalgia for the past is combined with a tasteful recall of older styles and a romanticized community ideal. Based on small-town virtues, the model avoids, rather than engages, current social realities. *Photos of Seaside, Florida, and Kentlands, Maryland, courtesy of the architects.*

Prozac age: Potemkin villages for dysfunctional families," Muschamp calls it. This restricted and rigidly controlled design, while charming to the eye, evades the issue and desirability of diversity and the city's "historic role as the matrix of experiment and innovation."[1]

No one denies that mythmaking is a legitimate function of architecture. The line between sentimental unreality and nostalgic idealism, between planning professionalism and shrewd marketing, is increasingly blurred, however, and that, too, is in the American tradition. With considerably less nostalgia and the immense pragmatism of ruthless land development, many of the new communities of the nineteenth-century West were laid out in railroad offices as part of profitable railroad expansion, complete with town and street names. Even at the highest national and idealistic level, the selection of a suitable architecture for the new democracy was a conscious choice by Thomas Jefferson: romantic classicism, imported from France, a new style for a nation without an image to define it. Small, white wooden temples with smoking chimneys multiplied across the land. As the years passed, the accretions of actuality and the alchemy of time supplied substance and character to invented and borrowed forms. What was arbitrary and artificial at the start was naturalized by the processes of use, growth, adaptation, and evolutionary change. These products of destiny and desire, financial opportunism, and, occasionally, of art, have become real places with acquired diversity to meet needs beyond the control of restrictive stylistic covenants; they have a real style of their own.

There is a direct line from the historical invention of place in the American past to that quintessential and most universal of modern American inventions, the theme park. When place becomes story, or snatches of story, designed as an appealing visual narrative, when the primary concerns are stage setting and role playing, anything is possible. When the story line is selected, and everything is coordinated to reinforce the illusion of reality—or of the borrowed reality—the result is, as their creators and marketers say, a "themed" package. Unlike those earlier borrowed styles or new communities, there is no attempt to create a functional plan in sociological or urbanistic terms. The image, and the intention, are

1 Herbert Muschamp, "Can New Urbanism Find Room for the Old?" *New York Times*, June, 1996.

limited and static; if anything is added or dropped, it is done not to accommodate growth and change in a living organism, but to supply more popular and profitable entertainment features. The themed package sells.

The theme park is a singular and significant product of our time and a distinctly American contribution to world culture and human experience. The theme can be geographical or historical, secular or religious, fictional or fantastic; it can invent worlds of the past, present, or future. There are parks for marine and animal life, domestic or wild, and a genre on the increase, the participatory theme park with hands-on, simulated experiences in simulated natural settings or site-and-story rides in re-created movie back lots. The high-tech adventure park has replaced the old amusement park, with the rides upgraded to hair-raising trips through the programmed "dangers" of crocodiles and volcanoes that can be enjoyed safely in parts of the country that have never seen either. Space trips and pirate journeys offer thrill-packed computerized alternatives. Moreover, the suave production and sleek technology employed have been appropriated by purveyors of education and culture in everything from church services to museum displays.

Salem's seventeenth-century Witch House, its sense of authenticity already diminished by its location on a traffic-assaulted street corner, is further compromised by a visitor-friendly entrance canopy and café curtains. *Photo, Edward O. Nilsson.*

On-site history (real history, so to speak), can be revisited with the same kind of artifice. Where witches were actually imprisoned and put to torture and trial, in Salem, Massachusetts, the experience can be had in the same setting with *son et lumière*, live actors or programmed mannequins, suitably enhanced by smoke and screams. By far the most moving and evocative experience in Salem is none of this; it is a small, silent, eloquently designed, parklike memorial to the witch trials that evokes more genuine emotion and brings one closer to this strange and tragic episode in the American past than any of the stagy re-creations.

This prizewinning example of environmental sculpture, the work of architect James Cutler and artist Maggie Smith, uses stone and trees to enormous effect. The design is simplicity itself. A rectangular, roomlike space is enclosed with low granite walls, open at the far end to the adjoining historic cemetery where some of the most active participants in the seventeenth-century trials, including a presiding judge, lie buried. Set into the beautifully laid, rugged walls are slab benches of rough stone, each with the incised name of a convicted "witch" together with the date of the trial and manner

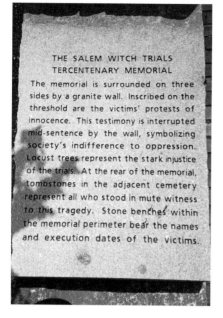

THE SALEM WITCH TRIALS
TERCENTENARY MEMORIAL
The memorial is surrounded on three
sides by a granite wall. Inscribed on the
threshold are the victims' protests of
innocence. This testimony is interrupted
mid-sentence by the wall, symbolizing
society's indifference to oppression.
Locust trees represent the stark injustice
of the trials. At the rear of the memorial,
tombstones in the adjacent cemetery
represent all who stood in mute witness
to this tragedy. Stone benches within
the memorial perimeter bear the names
and execution dates of the victims.

The competition-winning design for
the Witch Trials Tercentenary
Memorial in Salem, Massachusetts:
A serenely walled and landscaped
outdoor room where the protestations of innocence of the condemned
and the dates and manner of their
execution are engraved on somber
slabs of granite, evoking the real
presence of history far better than the
surrounding tourist sound and hype.
James Cutler, architect; Maggie
Smith, visual artist.

of execution, from hanging to "pressed to death." The walls of this outdoor room are flanked by rows of black locusts. Carved into the granite floor, as one enters, are the victims' protestations of innocence. How feeble and glaringly inappropriate are sound tracks and animatronics in the face of this eloquent silence. There is a powerful presence here. This is a place where history hurts.[2]

No subject is immune to reinvention. The battle that ensued in 1994 when Disney proposed a theme park with its own interpretation of American history close to the Manassas battlefield in Virginia was almost as violent as the Civil War clash itself. History was to be edited, animated, and merchandised, for a price and with appropriate by-products. The withdrawal of the scheme, achieved by a well-orchestrated opposition on historical and environmental grounds, was probably due as much to the softening of the real estate market as to considerations of authenticity, suitability, or the damage to Disney's public image. Not at all coincidentally, this drop in the market made the timing bad for the residential and commercial developments that were part of the plan. The project was not immediately relocated, as expected; it isn't that easy to find a piece of prime land amenable to the auxiliary upscale construction that would have been the theme park's ultimate bonanza. And although it is heresy to say it, there were other reasons for the plan's unpopularity; not everyone is enamored enough of Disney's product to welcome its version of American history.

The themed scenarios of these entertainment parks provide a controlled environmental experience where the whole family can share feelings of shock, nostalgia, or the sense of uplift to be derived from some suitably dramatic environmental, historical, or cultural information. There is a substantial literature about the phenomenon of theme parks and their surging popularity that ranges from rapt endorsement to scathing criticism. The American architect Charles Moore's early observations about the substitution of Disneyland and places like it for traditional, shared, public space provided an essential understanding of something unique to

2 We have only recently rediscovered the powerful memorial qualities of the wall with the Vietnam Veterans Memorial (1982), Maya Lin's competition-winning monument that is one of Washington's most visited landmarks and most moving experiences. The wall carries messages with a directness that even the most heroic sculpture cannot equal. The competition for the Salem Witch Trials Tercentenary Memorial was held in 1991. Its small scale creates an intimate and personal experience of singular impact. It is open year-round, twenty-four hours a day.

American life. It also gave them an instant iconic status. But Moore's equally significant point was that there was now a price of admission, literally, for this once free form of public social congress.[3] Beyond paying admission at the gate, however, today's theme park sells everything except the pig's squeak. The "all-inclusive" price of admission is only preliminary to the aggressive availability of any salable item devised by the mind of man, woman, or imagineer, resolutely integrated into every featured attraction. They get you, in every way possible, coming and going.

But the park itself is more than an entertainment cash cow; it is the centerpiece of the surrounding land that is the crux of Disney's long-term investment policy. Although little public attention is paid to this aspect of Disney's business strategy—and those who flock to its entertainments rarely know or care—the theme park is the decoy for real estate deals and development projects of enormous potential profitability. The theme park as focus and opportunity for land development is one of the most lucrative of all investments. Ostensibly (and practically) the surrounding land is bought and held by the park's owners for expansion, including its own hotels and resorts. But the big payoff comes with office complexes, malls, housing developments, and other commercial construction owned, operated, sold or leased, leased back, retained or disposed of by any number of elaborate real estate mechanisms. This is all perfectly legitimate strategy and very good business practice; no one does it better than Disney. How it must have hurt to give up that upscale Virginia location, beyond any loss of educational or amusement mission.

Far out front in these ventures is the Disney Development Company, formed in 1984 by the Walt Disney Company "to plan, develop and operate real estate and new business opportunities compatible with Disney's entertainment mission."[4] It is quite remarkable that the motivating mechanism behind the Disney universe is still perceived as something warm, fuzzy, and fun; the irresistibility of some goofily endearing, brilliantly conceived (if you will) cartoon characters giving joy to the world. What is really operating here are some brilliantly conceived, hard-nosed

3 CHARLES W. MOORE, "You Have To Pay for the Public Life," *Perspecta, the Yale Architectural Journal*, 9/10, (1965), 57–65.

4 Description from Disney literature distributed with promotional material for Celebration.

marketing ideas and corporate investment strategies of almost unlimited potential.[5]

I am the first to admit that my own recreational needs and tastes are different from those of many of my fellow Americans. I was not brought up on Disney; nothing at home wore ears. My fantasies came from those red, blue, and other classic, color-coded children's books of fairy tales animated by Disney; considerable has been lost in the cartoon translation. John Tenniel's black-and-white illustrations for *Alice in Wonderland* and *Through the Looking-Glass* of a dour, formally dressed White Rabbit in a proper waistcoat (no toothy Bugs Bunny, he), a ferociously angry Red Queen, a decidedly odd tea party, and a wickedly grinning Cheshire Cat looming large in the sky have always stayed with me; I have indelible memories of an uncuddly walrus (who didn't talk funny) and a far from avuncular old Father William standing on his head. These creatures existed in a shadowed and slightly sinister, untechnicolored mise-en-scène in a child's mind, wonderfully delineated images full of fright and delight that have not faded with time. They were definitely not cute. They were very, very good. Lewis Carroll's Alice was followed by A. A. Milne's lighter and sweeter Christopher Robin and Winnie the Pooh, who was much cuddlier but still free of grotesque distortion. (Pooh has not escaped: smoothed, sweetened, and softened, i.e., spoiled)

I confess that I am part of a small and somewhat bullied group (we dare not speak our name) never enchanted by the Disney style, even as children. In this time of minority entitlements I claim the right to remain unenchanted. I was not just put off by the chewing gum-like, whiplash draftsmanship—a style still perpetuated and perpetrated in the horrible marquee of Disney's Fifth Avenue store in New York—I actively disliked the classic Disney chases in the movie shorts starring Mickey, Goofy, Donald Duck, and Company; the aggressive, noisy animation, hairbreadth escapes, and rubbery caricatures made me acutely uncomfortable. As for mice, I preferred Krazy Kat's friend Ignatz. By inclination and profession, however, I am a responsible, and responsive, consumer of all

5 This happy land turns less than benign when behind-the-scenes information on how it all works is requested. As writers find who compare notes, some not-so-friendly rules are strictly enforced, which includes the classic stonewalling and runaround routines. Particularly, it seems, for those writing books even the most routine material is off-limits; the dance goes from the press office to the legal department, where it dead-ends. It helps a lot to have a friend with connections.

aspects of art and culture; as a critic, I have never written seriously about anything that I have not experienced firsthand. I began to feel, as minorities often do, left out. I knew that I was out of touch and probably always had been. It was clear that I had to start over, at the beginning, with Disneyland, and that I had to go with an open mind, ready, like the friends of Tinker Bell, to believe. I had high expectations that I would finally catch the magic.

My anticipation was colored by all I had read and heard about the high level of the technological and creative skills that I would find. What I did find was uniformly ordinary and well landscaped. I was not quite prepared for the numbing oversell. Unlike some critics, I was neither outraged nor indignant, just disappointed and depressed. I went with a good friend, a native Californian who grew up with Disneyland, loves it, and turns into a delighted child again with every ride through Pirates of the Caribbean or the Haunted Mansion. Her pleasure is palpable and catching. She has a young son with a wardrobe of make-believe clothes from Superman to Captain Hook; he dons the character with the costume and insists that everyone else fit into the scenario of the day. Still, he has reached the stage of knowing, or wanting to know, what is what. "Is this real or is it pretend?" he will ask, a question that many adults, lulled by docudramas and authentic reproductions, have stopped asking. It is also a question that raises problematic issues of the character and relationship of art and experience to the pseudo-environment and factoid history.

I am not too old for fantasy; I fell hard for Disney's tiny toy men turning the handles in the popcorn machines, each dressed to match his own theme area, busy making what my companion informed me was the best popcorn in the world. But something kept intruding into my willing suspension of disbelief, my desire to share the delight that this avowed fountainhead of fantasy works so hard to provide. What bothered me was not the intentions, or the unreality, as much as the nature of almost everything involved. I was appalled that the vaunted high level of technology supports such a low level of imagination and design. Disneyland is expertly engineered, standardized mediocrity, endlessly, shamelessly consumerized, a giant shill operation with a Mickey Mouse facade.

The huckstering is relentless. Behind every fake front, at every entrance and exit of every feature, something is inescapably for sale —refreshments, related merchandise, or concession goods—all of

Main Street, U.S.A. (Walt Disney World) Old-fashioned, small town America, romanticized, bowdlerized, and commercialized, for a timeless and universal appeal.
© *Disney Enterprises, Inc.*

which goes like the popcorn. I don't know why this should surprise me, except that I had expected something better. I am part of a nation of shoppers, and I should have realized that not even heart-stopping art or mind-blowing originality, assuming one could find it, would substitute for the big buy. I headed hopefully for Alice in Wonderland, looking for something that obviously wasn't there. I liked the idea of the teacup ride, and I plunged into the Mad Hatter Shop, a natural opportunity for fun and whimsy (where better than hats?). But like all other merchandise, they were DI (Disney issue) dull. Repeatedly, the word "cheesy" came to mind —but not cheap; things seemed wildly overpriced. Just in case a shopping opportunity may have been missed, however, a giant store of all-Mickey merchandise offers a last chance before the final exit to part with real money or Disney dollars (purchased with real money at the gate, on the assumption that it will surely be parted with). If you have everything else, you may still need the ice trays that freeze Mickey-shaped cubes; here a kind of demented imagination for banal kitsch has been working overtime.

One leaves with a sense of truly awesome commercial overkill. The sums being raked in—quite aside from the exorbitant entrance fee—must be more awesome still; a family of four can't walk past the entrance gate without handing over a hundred dollars or more, and I am assuming two overage grandparents and two underage children for discounted, minimal cost. If they show signs of sticker shock (you get a hand stamp for reentry, which ostensibly helps), they are informed that everything inside is free. This turns out not to be true of food, refreshment, or souvenirs, which can add up to some pretty magic numbers. But, in a festival mood, who counts? In the tradition of the carnival and midway, the fleecing is fabulous; but the genius of the operation is that it is all legitimate— you get what you pay for—and cheerfully self-inflicted.

Far more distressing than the unrelenting commercialism is the uninspired design. True, there is a consistent "house" style; it is both dated and deadly. Perhaps that is at the heart of my inability to accept the concept or find pleasure in it. I felt assaulted by the tackiness of the ideas, their execution, and the products. Most disheartening of all in a place built on and dedicated to imagination is the lack of it. Any magic derives from what is left of the far-from-simple wonder of timeless fairy tales or from the bowdlerized (Disneyfied) classic children's stories, so rich in the original that any residue can still intrigue young minds. But there is an awful descent from the sentimentalized and expertly animated movie versions to the plastic banalities of the amusement park.

My most severe disappointment was Main Street, U.S.A., the popular feature with which Disneyparks open, those cute Victoriana knockoffs and other clichés replicated wherever Disney builds. With all the marvelous source material available, one wonders how this knee-jerk version came about. Any architect or historian could do better than these obvious architectural knockoffs. What a missed opportunity! The smaller scale of the upper stories is frequently cited as a brilliant design ploy; Walt Disney is credited with the discovery that this gave a toylike, playful quality to the setting that people enjoyed. But this clever feature is neither the giant stroke of transforming genius that Disney cultists claim, nor does it offset a barren set of references totally devoid of the stylistic mix available in any American small town, where the real thing still exists. A lot was demolished or disguised after World War II, when so many small towns, anxious to "modernize," were uniformly "Kawneered" by that manufacturer's prefabricated panels, which papered over Main Streets across the country in aqua and shrimp pink. But much was only covered up, not destroyed, and the original period facades are being increasingly rediscovered and restored.

The argument one hears repeatedly for these impoverished formulas is that Disneyland is for children, and adult standards are irrelevant. It works, doesn't it, so why knock it or change it? If that were true, we would never have had the marvelously imaginative children's books, with their elegant writing and distinctive art, from *Alice in Wonderland* to *Dr. Seuss*. Or we are given the rather threatening populist argument (up against the wall, you elitists!) that because so many like it the way it is, criticism is churlish or unnecessary. But hack is simply not good enough. The products are virtually inescapable, and all alike. The cocoon of copyrighted sameness wraps childhood around the world. With claims of universal relevance, and unarguably universal impact, why should anyone be shortchanged by the quality of design?

The Disney experience is offered, as we say, to children of all ages and, advertised as family fare, it includes quite grown-up restaurants with prices to match for the adults. The fact that the formulas haven't worked as well for Disney in France may or may not reflect a higher proportion of adults or adult thinking. The initial failure (attendance is supposed to have improved subsequently) could have been the accident of a depressed economy at the time of its opening in 1990, or the high cost of tickets could have discouraged those who traditionally know the value of a franc and prefer to bring their own food and drink rather than be set up for an overpriced hamburger and a nonstop hard sell. EuroDisneyland has not exactly been the smash hit that was expected although it is now claimed to be in the black. There were marketing misjudgments, but there could be a different message that nobody wants to hear.

For every criticism, however, there is a counterargument, and, as each flags, another takes its place. First, we were told that Disney's advanced technology, expert management, and shrewd understanding of the popular mind and taste put the planning and design professions in the shade. Architects and urbanists, thus discarded, along with their more traditional and serious ideas, were quick to see the light. The Disney model was to replace and revolutionize architectural and planning theory and practice. (It hasn't, and it won't) We were also told that criticisms were irrelevant because the Disney product, good or bad, is clearly what people want. That begs the question of how people know what they want without options, including products and opportunities they have neither seen nor experienced. The latest argument has a more sophisticated ring. We are told that it is a little naive and certainly too simple (in the pejorative sense) to judge Disney, or theme park culture, against reality or to measure the product against the sources that are being cannibalized; everyone knows that the process of editing and interpreting has created a product and a reality all its own, to be judged, so to speak, by its own standards. Comparisons with anything else, we are told rather patronizingly, miss the point. The thing has become itself, autonomous and beyond argument, its own reality. There is nothing to denigrate if you look at it this way. One can be knowing, amused, and tolerant and a little superior to those uptight spoilers who think the result is any less wonderful than presliced American cheese. These apologists exploit Eco's observation that the fake has acquired the aura of reality, while ignoring his corollary argument that the copy has corrupted the source and the original artifact.

As Baudrillard has put it—for heretics and unbelievers, of course: "What is offered in Disneyland is a parody of the imagination…[a] deep-frozen infantile world…Embalmed and pacified…"[6] Another

6 Jean Baudrillard, Simulations, Paul Foss, Paul Patton, and Philip Beitchman, trans. (New York: Semiotext(e), Inc., 1983), 23–24

critic, Edward W. Soja, looks on its achievements with less than reverence: "Today the simulations of Disneyland seem almost folk-loric, crusty incunabula of a passing era."[7] EPCOT Center in Walt Disney World, intended in Disney's original concept to be a model of the world of the future, has sidestepped the promised vision of a community based on technological revolution for a more conventional showcase of corporate and commercial wonders—shades of the old world's fairs.[8]

A more recent (1991-1993) themed construction aimed at an equally broad audience, Universal Studios' CityWalk in Los Angeles, suggests that it is possible to raise one's sights, to create an illusionistic experience through a greater use of talent and stylish imagination. CityWalk is a shopping, eating, socializing Main Street built to connect Universal's movie theaters to its "back lot" rides. It uses artful and even daring design—isn't that really the bottom line of invention?—able to match everyone's personal receptors on any number of levels.

A useful comparison can be made between CityWalk and an addition to Disneyland, Mickey's Toontown, designed at about the same time. Toontown's cartoon version of a Main Street for cartoon characters is a spin-off of *Who Framed Roger Rabbit.* Caricatured facades are bunched together to form a crazy-quilt streetfront that neither quotes amusingly (CityWalk does that on a very high level), nor refers nostalgically, nor invites imaginatively. The overriding creative and comic idea here is no straight lines. There are funny bulbous columns, tipsy Tyrolean flower boxes, and other tired top-of-the-head touches. Nothing intrigues as illusion or opens the mind to a magical unknown. The big treat is to get on a distorted Jolly Trolley and racket across the "street" in a foreshortened ride.

As urban caricature, this is a dismal distance from the wonderful cockeyed universe of Red Grooms, for example, where art, fantasy, and commentary meet on so many levels of wit and meaning.

7 Edward W. Soja, "Inside Exopolis: Scenes from Orange County," in Michael Sorkin, ed., Variations on a Theme Park (New York: Hill and Wang, 1992), 101.

8 General Motors plans a major overhaul of its EPCOT exhibit "from a marketing perspective," to reflect "broader shifts in sales strategies…It's all part of creating a marketing architecture to support individual car and truck lines." The vision of the world of the future reduced to "an opportunity to interact with a customer, or a potential customer, for 25 minutes." *New York Times*, February 13, 1996.

previous pages: Universal Studios' CityWalk in Los Angeles, an invented Main Street, uses expert architectural parodies as facades for real activities from boutiques and bookstores to university extension courses. The Jon Jerde Partnership. *Photos, A.L. Huxtable.*

Even my Disney-enthusiast friend feels let down by Toontown. It lacks the delight of the kind of make-believe that expands the sense of myth, romance, and adventure that fascinated her as a child and still does. This is a flat, funny-paper bore, a concrete catch basin that becomes Toontorture on a hot, crowded day.

The fact that CityWalk is witty and sophisticated has not kept it from being an instant success. It suffers from cartoon excess, but that is the accepted idiom; restrained understatement is not a component of today's pop sensibility. I doubt if those who like Disneyland like CityWalk any less. They probably make no distinction, but that is not the point. You certainly see the same kind of visitors in both. It helps that CityWalk is being used for its own sake—much like a promenade or a city square, albeit with an entrance fee—as well as a way to get people from the theaters to the rides. What is happening here is the morphing of theme park into shopping center.

CityWalk is hard-surfaced and very urban and full of real and imaginary style. Its designers, the Jerde Partnership of Los Angeles, have gone beyond the firm's specialty of shopping malls and the expert marketing of hokum imagery (themes), to create a place that is wildly referential and genuinely entertaining. Don't expect subtlety —you must prefer things bright and loud. But the artificial setting serves real food, from Wolfgang Puck's pizzas to Häagen-Dazs ice cream, and there is a real bookstore that offers tables for browsing, conversation and real espresso. A variety of functions that one would hope to find on such a street are contained in a setting that consists of a pastiche of design references to real buildings and places that emphasizes clever artifice. Each of these instant buildings has a real purpose, clearly defined, as opposed to Disney's fake fronts housing redundant souvenir shops; behind these facades are real places and uses, from specialty stores to UCLA extension courses. This is a kind of successful crossover stage-set urbanism that delivers.

There are some very good things here, including two of the most original small urban fountains I have seen. A tiny, mock seashore is suggested by a timed, repeated rush of flat, shallow water breaking over a row of rocks with a rhythmical swish, in front of a clothing store called the Current Wave. This street surf made me do something I have done not in Disneyland but at the Niki de Saint Phalle–Jean Tinguely fountain at the Pompidou Center in Paris: laugh with surprise and delight. At a Mexican cantina, thin sheets of water barely wash flat squares of sidewalk bordering a stone cube that periodically releases plumes of steam. You can stand in or walk through the water, but a sign warns that running or roughhousing are not allowed. CityWalk apparently attracts a more unpredictable urban mix than the sanitized pseudostreets of Disneyland.

Architecture buffs will recognize skillful takeoffs on the work of Venturi and Scott Brown, Frank Gehry, Richard Meier, and Frank Israel—a mélange of international celebrity architects and the local Los Angeles avant-garde—all condensed into a lively amalgam of California style with palm trees (real). Others will not, but it won't matter. There is something for everyone; it can be enjoyed at many levels. What counts is the conceptual quality of design of this invented urbanism; the effects are rich with references that take off and double back on real sources. For whatever it signifies, my City Walk pasta primavera was really primavera. My Disney pasta primavera salad was a virtually veggie-free mass of sodden soup noodles on a magic mountain of lettuce. It was served in a restaurant called the Blue Bayou, so dark that it was hard to see that its mysterious, watery ambience came from being wedged neatly between the Pirates of the Caribbean waterway and New Orleans Square. I suppose you could call this expeditious transition a brilliant example of the highly touted planning. Sophisticated art and technology are more in evidence at CityWalk.

As a consumer of contemporary culture, I am turned off as frequently as I am exhilarated, but I accept the trade-off as reality. These artificial places have established themselves securely in American life and are here to stay. In the convincing face of their utility and popularity, one would have to be blind or a willful fool not to accept this. But it would take a fool, or a total innocent, to have no discomfort about them. They were, of course, invented by Disney and done first by Disney, and much has been learned from Disney; what hasn't been stolen has been copied. Disney alumni have carried the know-how with them, and in some places, they are doing it better, or others are doing it better. There is the prospect of real competition in the Land of Let's Pretend. Both Walt Disney World and Universal Studios are expanding constantly and introducing new enterprises in Florida.[9] The latter's movie-based theme

9 Buoyed by what it says is the booming success of Universal CityWalk in Los Angeles, MCA Inc. announced that it is building and even bigger version of the entertainment complex in Orlando. This complex, called the E-Zone, will have twelve acres of restaurants, bars, theaters, nightclubs, and shops adjoining the Universal City theme park. *Los Angeles Times*, November 16, 1995.

park is modeled on *Jurassic Park,* long the most successful movie of all time. The Universal Studios complex, conceived as a multibillion-dollar joint American-Japanese-British financial venture, will be complete with resort hotels.

Mickey is immortal, but that may not be enough. Other functions of these complexes are increasingly important in terms of services and entertainment offered and time and dollars spent. These constantly expanding features have far surpassed the original amusement purposes for which the parks were planned. (And they are planned, if only in shrewd psychomarketing terms, if you wonder whatever happened to planning.) There is no lack of capital to support these make-believe, made-from-scratch environments; what appears to be missing is any inclination to enlist those seemingly risky ingredients—imagination and excellence—of both design and product. It is a truism of American business practice that standards are raised only when competition demands it. The kind of "imagineering" complacency that leaves design dead in the water could be an eventual disaster as the market becomes more and more saturated and the public has more to choose from. A changing Disney management could force the issue, although it seems that efforts may be concentrated on animated movies with the enormously and instantly profitable spin-off of cassette sales. But the theme park will still be the bait for land development and the draw for the monster shopping mall.

I was supposed to follow my trip to Disneyland with a visit to Walt Disney World, to see how much better everything is being done in Florida—state of the art, and all that—but my masochistic impulses are limited; I cannot make myself go. Even if there is a lot more whizbang technology, the premises and style will be the same. My California friend and reliable Disney enthusiast, for whom the Florida pilgrimage is a ritual experience, assures me it is pretty much more of the same—but supersame, so to speak, sort of like Ronald Reagan's reaction to trees: once you've seen one you've seen them all. An architect who sits on the Disney board tells me that the place is packed with stunning advances and informs me that I must have the full treatment to be able to "attack from strength," as he puts it. The idea is that everything has been improved and/or perfected. That is an extremely depressing thought. You could carry the Disney philosophy and formulas straight into cyberspace, and they probably have by now, but for me it would still be cybersausage, no matter how they slice it. The marvels of simulated places leave me cold when measured against the miracle of the survivals that document a real society.

The famous underground world that services the Disney illusion, universally praised as such a technological achievement and of particular interest to the architectural press, is off-limits to writers; requests to see it are treated with profound suspicion. Pictures of the tunnels beneath the platform, where scurrying Mickeys have been known not to smile, are routinely bootlegged by architectural publications. There seems to be some feeling that the stardust might blow away if the world knew what makes the world of Disney work. This cheery land is not about to be demystified by any breach in security—not that offenders are flogged or thrown into dungeons under Sleeping Beauty's Castle. Everyone just gets the same runaround and standard handouts. When my-friend-the-Disney-board-member interceded, that brought an invitation and a book of publicity clips of unalloyed praise that could kill an ox. In any event, I define wit and fantasy differently: as a freeing of the mind and spirit to explore unknown places, rather than a handshake from some unconvincingly costumed actors in a totally predictable and humdrum context. I stand on my nonconforming-minority rights.

Wherever one chooses to go, it becomes very clear that something else is being sold in these themed environments besides the omnipresent merchandise, and it is equally evident why this works so well. We hear a lot about how clean and safe these places are, how unthreatening, how homogenized and comfortable in racial and ethnic terms. You see an enormous mix of people who seem to share some common denominator of taste and experience, excluding, of course, the downtrodden or antisocial types that are obviously not wanted (the roughhousers). There are those families that seem to bubble out of the wellsprings of Middle America, where T-shirts communicate with more and more recondite and commercial messages and athletic shoes achieve awesome proportions and fluorescent complexity. Women in improbable, spray-rigid hairdos and permanent-press, pastel pantsuits or shorts are straight out of Saul Steinberg's gallery of Amazons. And there are the young, of every shape and style in every make of jeans and sweatpants, and, of course, the children, from babies in backpacks and strollers to teenagers.

What all these visitors are sharing is leisure time. And what they are getting is not just a two-hour movie, or a morning at a museum, or a tour through re-created or invented history, after which they must find a place to eat or sleep, with attendant uncertainties and potential disappointments. They are getting eight to twelve full hours or more—depending on the season and how long the place is open—of absolutely certain, predictable, wholesome, undisturbing entertainment. (Universal Studios decided not to show its ghetto-set film *Poetic Justice* in its CityWalk complex.) Those who come, stay for at least a full day or several days if they choose to, eliminating the problem of not knowing how to pass the time or where to go or what to do. And at the beginning and end of it—and in the middle if they want, with a pass for reentry—they are whisked by tram, bus, or other waiting and available transport to a hotel (or right into the hotel by monorail at Walt Disney World). There they will be equally taken care of, often with the fantasy or "theme" continued—everything still predictable, and with still more goods for sale.

This is a formula that is simply unbeatable. Entertain people, take care of them, offer them no unpleasant or unexpected surprises—but, most of all, occupy them totally, for a length of time, and in a way never before possible. All the theorizing and hand-wringing about Disney and the theme park phenomenon misses the point. This is so easy, so time-filling, so complete, so prepackaged; nothing to do beyond buying the plane tickets; no strange language or customs or hostile environments; above all, no decisions to make. Considering the convenience and the all-consuming activities, even the exorbitant cost really doesn't seem to matter. These places fill a need that is not about to go away. It is not that people are voting for these enterprises in positive terms; they are simply responding to the satisfaction of a need in the most passive way. The identification of the need was easy; the genius is in the merchandising.

The prospects are unlimited and golden. Walt Disney World's addition of Yacht Club and Beach Club resorts extended its successful theme park hotels from overnight stopovers to a new concept of full, themed vacations for longer visitor stays and more tourist dollars. Detailed throughout to evoke the opulent, late-nineteenth-century verandahed wooden hotels of the old-money, upper-crust, East Coast summer colonies like Bar Harbor, Maine, the Florida re-creations are made of whole cloth—or, rather, whole plastic: glued sawdust clapboards and fiberglass balustrades to withstand the tropical humidity. And while Ralph Lauren (in another superbly understood game of fashionable make-believe) may purvey the blazers and braid and perfectly pressed linens that are the dreamworld trappings of upper-class lifestyle needed to complete the fantasy, it is sneakered and T-shirted middle-class America that comes and pays the bills. But the point is illusion, not veracity. Never underestimate the remarkable skills expended on these ersatz wonders. And never underestimate the fact that they are enormously and endlessly profitable.

Like so much of America before it, these places have also been invented out of nothing and nowhere, in the traditional American way. (Not the least noticeable feature is the giant parking lot.) Because the genre is fruitful and multiplies, it is creating a new American landscape. But it goes beyond the invention of place in the older, more conventional sense, beyond the continental expansion and new communities of the past, and beyond the places to live and work produced by the laws of supply and demand. These are purely profit-making enterprises of a very special and limited kind; entertainment is their sole purpose and reason for being.

That makes them a curious model for anything at all, but particularly for those who claim them as inspiration for architectural or environmental design; what this does is reduce the planning of communities to the image of a cartoon Congeniality, U.S.A., with all the modern conveniences. Whatever lessons may be applicable, too much that matters is missing. But since nothing succeeds like success, and no image is more sought after, at a time of cataclysmic urban crime and decay, than the old-fashioned hometown with its neighborly front porches and backyards, the myths of a romanticized past are being saluted and adopted by both architects and builders, with pervasive and often surprising effects on the places where real life is lived.

The real now imitates the imitation. Towns are remaking themselves, and developments are casting themselves in the theme park image, given a stage-set presence from a look to a complete concept carried out to the last "authentic" touch. Orlando, the town closest to Walt Disney World, has taken it as its model. Restaurants and stores are routinely "themed." Dream-house subdivisions are "pastel agglomerations of arbitrary architecture, all behind secure walls"[10] in styles that are pure—or, rather, impure—selective fantasies. Orlando has been called a "new psychological frontier, a jumping-off place for a society that revels in the surface of things,

10 Priscilla Painton, "Fantasy's Reality," *Time*, May 27, 1991, p. 55.

CLASSICAL

VICTORIAN

COLONIAL REVIVAL

COASTAL

MEDITERRANEAN

FRENCH

even if deeper problems remain unaddressed."[11] At the same time that tax dollars paid for a Disney-inspired, squeaky-clean image, *Time* tells us, little was spent on the overcrowded school system. The color and fabric of Orlando's basketball team uniform were the subject of a diligent yearlong search of the sort usually undertaken for university presidents. The Florida Symphony Orchestra, headquartered in Orlando, has had to struggle to exist.

Population continues to swell as people move to Orlando to find their ideal world. "It's not clear where Disney World begins and ends," observes author John Rothchild.[12] "You kind of feel seduced away from reality," says a lawyer who is a twenty-year resident. "But…maybe *this* is reality."[13] He and many others would concur with Eco's conclusion that through adaptive simulation and inversion of values, the unreal has become the reality.

Reality is moot. A new town in Florida, planned and designed from scratch by the Disney Development Company, is simply and unashamedly called Celebration. This sublimely spurious hometown, as it is referred to in oneword Disneyspeak, is "perhaps like the one you grew up in—or maybe just wish that you had." It is to be "a new, old-fashioned hometown…reminiscent of Norman Rockwell images," the promotional brochure promises. The houses "will recall the gracious style and character of traditional Southern neighborhoods built prior to the 1940s…Greek Revival could meet Georgian and Regency on a classic American street… Mediterranean and French Country style homes will reflect the cosmopolitan flavor…All in harmony with nature." And, supposedly, with each other, even if they have never met on the same street or in real life before. If you had any doubt, politically correct architecture has arrived.

"Celebration." the brochure punctuates breathlessly. "A town that's bringing back a good idea and making it better. A whole new kind of lifestyle that's not new at all—just lost for a while. That fellow who said you can't go home again? He was wrong. Now you can come home. To Celebration. Your new hometown."[14] A little organ

11 Painton, 54.

12 Ibid., 55.

13 Ibid., 54.

14 From promotional brochure for Celebration.

music, please, while I weep for a past that never was; a future that is pure sales pitch, aimed at our most simplistic, xenophobic, and exclusionary instincts; and for those architects, with very good names indeed, who are designing this consummate fakery with consummate skill, without any innocence at all (and who may or may not cry all the way to the bank.) On second thought, I may just fwow up.

However, when you get past the saccharine hyperbole, the experts show their hand. The design standard set leaves the imagineers far behind. Here is an example of the wrong thing being done right. Enormously and alarmingly right. No stranger to either art or commerce, Disney CEO Michael Eisner has brought in top planning and architectural talents for a project clearly under his eye; even the promotional graphics have taken a cosmic leap upward since the preliminary announcement. The usual Disney schlockmeisters are nowhere to be found. Eisner has been quoted as seeing Celebration in the role of the prototype residential community of the future, an ideal in which psychological acumen, architectural expertise, brilliant business tactics, and marketing skill are equal partners. As chief planner, Jacquelin T. Robertson brings qualifications that include both domestic plans and projects for the shah of Iran, as well as a profound understanding, by both birth and professional practice, of the architectural and social traditions of Virginia and the South. The niceties will be observed. Robert A. M. Stern, also brings special qualifications to the task: an extensive historical knowledge and a roster of residential and institutional buildings that have transformed that knowledge into the architectural raiments of the rich and respectable or those who would be both. Intelligence and taste are in stunning supply; how they are being applied is instructive.

An official style book, suggestive of those of the early Republic which were used to instruct carpenter-builders and provide models for a "developing nation," has been created to establish basic house types, dimensions, and configurations that anyone building in the community must follow. Instruction has become regulation. All of the promised "looks" are there, but in selectively annotated and historically correct versions. Clever, "authentic" adaptation makes the ridiculous acceptable; this is a managed eclecticism of a seductive unreality that both blows and corrupts the mind. The planning is superior. Disney has been willing and able to provide the up-front money that developers lack or are unwilling to invest, and also to draw on the best and brightest ideas for the greatest amenity, from

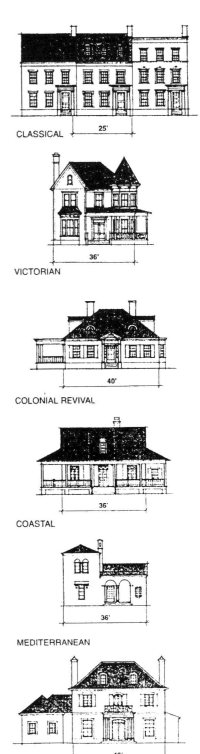

CLASSICAL

VICTORIAN

COLONIAL REVIVAL

COASTAL

MEDITERRANEAN

FRENCH

Approved house styles from the official pattern book of the Disney new town, Celebration, Florida. *Used by permission from Disney Enterprises, Inc.*

the quality and extent of the infrastructure to nature preserves and recreational facilities integrated with residential areas. Medical care and educational resources are stressed.

There is not going to be any way not to like Celebration. Its houses are already oversubscribed; among the buyers are top Disney personnel. Of course, one can expect the spoilers and the disgruntled to ask those same disturbing questions about unaddressed issues, diversity of population and style, sprawl and renewal, creativity and invention; about the death and life of great and small American cities and the decline of suburbia into dysfunction and decay, while we retreat behind exclusionary covenants and dictated design, and whether it just may not all eventually be dull beyond belief. This, at last, is the world according to Disney, the place to which we have all been heading. Is it any wonder that it's make-believe?

Celebration has sophisticated standards and a universal reach. It is the prototype for investment success. An assured profit potential exists in replicated residential developments of this type, far beyond anything Walt Disney could have imagined in the early days of the original simplistic entertainment formulas. The surrogate is now smoothly spurious, a perfect thing of its kind; this is instant yesterday with a cornucopia of improvements. Will there be an appropriate modern-house model, perhaps after the southern California style of Irving Gill? Or some version of Frank Lloyd Wright? Or does that come dangerously close to the edge of an Americana too exotic or unfamiliar? Let's face it, the Disney dream is terminally uptight. The whole town is probably copyrighted, down to the last picket fence. Everything else in the Disney empire is.

Something like this dreamworld already exists in a developer-bowdlerized form being delivered exponentially to buyers in upwardly mobile suburbia. Large houses on small lots reach for the props of drop-dead grandeur with bits of architectural and historical malapropism that play gross games with scale and style. Illusion is all—the illusion of affluence, the illusion of status, fed by fieldstone and wrought iron, when wood and shingles aren't enough. Split stairs curve up to double doors; startled oculi and vaguely Palladian windows ornament towers and dormers, all upstaged by enormous attached garages whose doors can be ordered in Gothic, Colonial, or Sunset motifs. Downsized French Provincial manor houses sink under massive mansards into a quarter acre of formal blacktop. This is not Hometown America; it is Upscale Never-Never Land with

In the world of dream-house McMansions, the preferred style is Grotesquely Grandiose. Unencumbered by architects or accuracy, developers offer a mind-boggling mix of Rapunzel towers and pretend Palladian, Jacuzzis and surround-sound. *Photos, Linda S. Williams.*

price tags in the millions to match. So much is lost in the editing and translation of real places into these pretentious parodies, and such a curious perversion of meaning and effect occurs on the way there and back, that the result, as Eco has so clearly put it, is a corruption of all the original sources, a distortion of reference and meaning that is its own cartoonland. These are the real Toontowns.

What has evolved is a new kind of developer house. In the same way that the ranch and split-level marked the postwar period, today's model is equally well defined. A two-story atrium entrance, with the omnipresent Palladenoid window above double doors, is designed specifically to impress. This grand entry leads to the Great Room, as it has been named by real estate sales offices, into which the kitchen–family room has evolved. In this large, all-purpose social and entertaining center, the latest equipment coexists with current decorating fashions. There is an exit to an outdoor deck (gone is the bugless screened porch of yesteryear) with a ritual gas or charcoal grill. A vestigial living room has become an extension of the Great Room, providing the opportunity to display more formal furnishings for "gracious living." Cathedral ceilings soar, topped with skylights galore.

Upstairs, another metamorphosis has taken place. Where once the traditional Colonial had four bedrooms and a bath at the top of the stairs, there is now a Master Suite, a closet- and mirror-lined dressing room of manorial proportions, connected to a large bedroom and a Jacuzzi-equipped bathroom of sybaritic splendor. Chrome- or gold-plated hardware pegs the price range and social scale, as does the number of garages on the main facade. Lesser bedrooms and additional baths vary according to the size of the house. The *Dynasty* image is from TV, much as the movies influenced taste in the 1940s/1950s. This is the drop-dead model for all those middle-class, do-it-yourself families that aspire to the symbols and comforts of the landed gentry (help's quarters are conspicuously lacking, as is help), combined with a dazzling display of the latest advances and highest styling in household equipment. It clearly responds to the way Americans live and dream today.

Still, we are creating these new suburbs and living in them, and they are clearly unlike any places we have made before. This, too, is a built landscape; it is the latest, most overwhelming chapter in a long tradition of artifice, which has included noble estates and formal or romantic landscapes and the ambitious projection of image on place through art. But this is the first vernacular building conceived apart from a received tradition, the first to break free from historical precedent to invent its own past. Divorced from the tradition it misappropriates, it has also become disconnected from all that is essential to the complex act of making an environment. It is not that anyone is intent on reinventing the wheel or the umbrella; both have simply been thrown away. So have the opportunities for innovative exploration to accommodate a way of life equally without precedents; there is no interest in imaginative and style-setting solutions appropriate to the radical reconstituting of the known and unknown that characterizes society today. The gesture most commonly made is the wrong one: the commissioning of "celebrity" architects to produce "signature buildings," themed trivia that only celebrates and compounds the degenerative process.

There is an important difference between today's thriving entrepreneurship of illusion and the impulses that invented identities for raw land and new communities in the past. Those earlier identities were an investment in character for rapidly growing new settlements, an attempt to establish some ready-made sense of place to define and speed development. Today's themed creations are not, and never will be, real places; they are not meant to be. They are made for the moment, instant environments intended to serve only as temporary, substitute events, conceived and carried out as places to visit in which novelty, experience, and entertainment are sold for immediate profit and a short period of time. They are based on proven, family-oriented entertainment formulas. To embrace their limited and exclusionary objectives is to forfeit the larger needs of place and society. To imitate their poverty of reference is to lose all we know about the past. To think that American cities can learn from them is to embrace the most dangerous illusion of all.

It does not help that American cities, towns, and landscapes have been consistently misunderstood. Traditionally, we do not like our cities very much; we have preferred the agrarian and the bucolic, the myth and romance of unspoiled, open space. Established taste and the official literature have dismissed or denigrated our cities, almost always for the wrong reasons; they have been compared pejoratively with the products of high European culture. The reality of the American city, short on order and long on jarring juxtapositions, has been deplored for its lack of harmony and beauty; native critics have consistently wrung their hands to cries of nostra culpa—we are the barbarians. Not until J. B. Jackson's brilliantly observant writings on the uses of the American city and the nature of suburbia and the highway strip as a response to American lifestyles were our eyes and minds opened to their form and meaning. Jackson's work in the 1950s defined the special character of the American city and landscape.[15] European visitors, steeped in a literary tradition of disdain, have now embraced what they once rejected.

The least we can ask, as we put large amounts of our money into corporate and speculative deep pockets, is that these artificial environments be well made: that imagination, creativity and quality, reference and relevance, should not be totally taboo, that all we have learned about urbanism and urbanity not be abandoned just when reinterpretation is not only possible and inevitable but essential. This is not the time to settle for the lowest common denominator of design. What is built now should add to the past with some sense of creative continuity, rather than devalue and deny the nature and worth of its antecedents. If the new American landscape is an escape from what has gone before, it is also part of it. It has its own realities of use and purpose, and the insistent reality of its existence. It has become a very real, unreal world.

The new vision of the American city was aided by the advent of pop art and its canonization in some intellectual circles. This led, in turn, to the celebration of truly spectacular American kitsch, including the awesome products of the themed environment—an American expression that continues to startle and delight with its outrageously energetic excesses. Not the least of the appeal of the pop art phenomenon to foreign visitors is the recognition and envy of a freedom and vitality absent from the more rigidly circumscribed—and, to a younger generation, exhausted—European cultural scene. Americans have been delighted to find that what was condemned as doggerel is now admired as free verse.

The newly identified pop landscape had tremendous appeal for born-again American architects seeking a way out of earnest modernist dogma. Postmodernists became giddy with it; they elevated its previously disdained urban aspects and artifacts to cult status. But some European observers, like André Corboz, have a

15 John Brinckerhoff Jackson's fresh eye and revealing insights on the American scene informed a series of enormously influential articles in *Landscape* in the 1950s, the magazine he founded and edited from 1951 until 1968. They were collected in 1970.

more measured view. The real America is neither to be loved nor despised, embraced or rejected: "I do not wish to depict the urban American reality as admirable but only…to demonstrate the instances where we have inappropriately applied our automatic criteria…" American cities are at last to be understood on their own terms. "To regret that Los Angeles is not Bruges or Viterbo is tantamount to playing gin rummy according to the rules of *belote*."[16] The rational European mind wants the rules clearly understood.

The fact is that Americans have thrown the rules away. We can, and do, build anything. We make no distinctions and apply no value judgments; the thing imitated is no better than the copy, and the reverse may be taken to be true. Las Vegas, an act of total artifice, pretends to be nothing but itself. "The essential risk," Corboz cautions, "is that the Hearst Castle will be mistaken for the Escorial."[17] Hardly. Even this astute observer missed the point. More likely, the Escorial will be appropriated by Disney. Today only the Disney version would be considered the real thing.

16 André Corboz, *Looking for a City in America: Down These Mean Streets a Man Must Go…* (Santa Monica: Getty Center for the History of Art and the Humanities, 1992), p. 55.

17 Ibid.

The Real Fake and the Fake Fake

previous pages: Dazzling new heights of updated illusion in the land of make-believe: New York, N.Y., a hotel and casino complex for Las Vegas. Joyce E. Orias, of Yates, Silverman.

left: Luxor Hotel, Las Vegas. Ancient Egypt in plastic and glass; only the desert is real. *Photo, Luxor Hotel.*

California, as usual, is the place that sets the trends and establishes the values for the rest of the country; like a slow ooze, California culture spreads eastward across the land. Only a Californian would have observed that it is becoming increasingly difficult to tell the real fake from the fake fake. All fakes are clearly not equal; there are good fakes and bad fakes. The standard is no longer real versus phony, but the relative merits of the imitation. What makes the good ones better is their improvement on reality.

The real fake reaches its apogée in places like Las Vegas where it has been developed to a high art form. As Robert Venturi, Denise Scott Brown, and Steven Izenour pointed out in their once controversial and now classic study, *Learning from Las Vegas*,[1] an entire vocabulary and language of architectural forms has been invented to satisfy new social, commercial, and cultural requirements and criteria. The giant billboard, the decorated shed, the use of moving light and color, continuous, competitive frontages of accelerating fantasy and novelty, all meant to attract the automobile moving at highway speed, seduce with visual wonders that lead to the gaming tables and hotels. The purpose is clear; the solution is dazzling. The result is completely and sublimely itself. What was once the gambling casino and is now being transformed into the "gaming resort" has become on its own terms, the real thing. The outrageously fake fake has developed its own indigenous style and lifestyle to become a real place.

John Jerde, the architect who is the established master of the modern shopping mall and all its clones and offspring, understands this phenomenon well. He defines his work as "placemaking", using a salesman's and psychologist's vocabulary and logic. In a spirit that is singularly American, places are now entertainment environments. They are also an urban design frontier where extraordinary things are happening. This can be seen as the American urbanistic avant garde, in the sense that it uses advanced technology and programmed perceptions for unprecedented solutions and sensations. The dream of pedestrianism, so valiantly and fruitlessly pursued by planners who have looked to the past or overseas to historic hill towns and plazas, has been aggresively naturalized; the social stroll has become a consumer experience in an instantly created, totally artificial setting like Universal CityWalk, which

1 ROBERT VENTURI, SCOTT BROWN, AND STEVEN IZENOUR, *Learning from Las Vegas: The Forgotten Symbolism of Architectural Form* (Cambridge, Mass.: MIT Press, 1972).

provides goods, services, education and amusement behind cleverly invented facades, or under a 1400-foot long, 90-foot high, curved space frame that spans Las Vegas's Fremont street—the original, now-dated Strip—to wrap the nighttime walker in a computer-generated sound and light show provided by 211 million lights and a 540,000-watt sound system.

Jerde's conversion of Fremont Street into "the Fremont Street Experience" is a perfect example of how the Las Vegas "drive-by" has become the "be-in," a people place rather than an automobile right-of-way. This upsets those nice theories of how Las Vegas and other highway attractions work and the lessons they supply. In practice, the Fremont Street Experience will need a lot more sophisticated and design-wise programming to live up to its potential as "a linear urban theater for pedestrians along the city's familiar icon and historic heart…"[2] Yes, Virginia, Las Vegas has a historic heart; you are too young to remember, but Fremont Street was invented and incorporated in 1905. More than seventy years old now, and getting a little tired, it is part of historic America along with Williamsburg and more recent landmarks like Route 66, the Mom and Pop motel, and MacDonald's earliest golden arches. The street is still evolving in a uniquely American way. As Corboz would caution, don't mistake Las Vegas for Monte Carlo; a singular confluence of desire, flash, and the big sell has created its unique character and destiny. This is the real, real fake, at the highest and loudest level of illusionistic artifice. It can, and should, be understood and enjoyed for what it is, by those with a taste for it. For those who prefer to study its wonders at a more Olympian level, it must be understood on its own terms.

Since gambling has been renamed gaming (another triumph of still another uniquely American phenomenon, public relations), and thus cleansed of all pejorative connotations and rendered euphemistically harmless, it has emerged at the top of the list of America's favorite pastimes. Las Vegas may have begun as a thoroughly adult, mob headquarters off-limits to minors; today places like Las Vegas and Atlantic City (one offers the desert and the other the ocean to those who venture outside) are being touted as family vacation spots. It has finally all come together: the lunar theatrical landscape of the Strip and the casino hotels, the amusement park and the shopping mall, themed and prefabricated, available as a

Fremont Street, Las Vegas, as updated by the Jerde Partnership: the controlled, computerized environment. *Photo, Timothy Hursley.*

2 JERDE, JON. Description in informational presentation.

The Forum Shops, Caesars Palace, Las Vegas. The family that games together, shops together, in a Roman-Rococo mall with triumphal arches, cascading fountains, and computerized sunsets. *Photos: Jeff Gayle, courtesy of the Forum Shops at Caesars.*

packaged vacation for all. The innocent inventions of Morris Lapidus, the Miami hotels of the 1950s—his blatantly, almost endearingly faux Fontainebleau gilded glamour and sluggish crocodiles in the equally faux jungle pool under the Americana's lobby stairs—have become the breathstopping extravaganzas of Caesars Palace with its heroic styrofoam statuary and the Luxor's giant Sphinx and mirror-glass pyramid.

Nor has the tradition of knockout effects originally developed for long-distance viewing been dishonored. New heights of drop-dead style and automated illusion are being reached.[3] The design of a hotel and casino complex called New York, New York is a pastiche of New York's famous skyscrapers—the Empire State Building, Chrysler Building, Seagram, CBS and AT&T form a collage of pinstriped towers for a wonderfully improbable facade. In front of this mirage-mélange is a dotty row of New York landmarks, side by side, almost holding hands—Grant's Tomb, the Soldiers and Sailors Monument, Ellis Island with the Statue of Liberty centered, front and forward in a reflecting pool, the United Nations, Grand Central, the Brooklyn Bridge and the cast-iron Haughwout Store (a dead giveaway that some real New York architecture buffs are at work), are all improbably and wonderfully laced with the airy, looping curves of a giant roller coaster. The designers, the Las Vegas firm of Yates-Silverman, Inc, with Joyce E. Orias, a graduate of the Jerde office, in charge of the project, have perfected the spirit of informed ludicrousness and outer-edge spectacle that mark the best of these undertakings.

Who needs Monte Carlo? Certainly not those families seeking a fun-filled experience, walking the Strip, much as they walked the Atlantic City boardwalk earlier in the century in search of entertainment. The family that games together, plays together, and stays together. The shopping malls and theme parks that have joined the slots have not let down anyone's fevered expectations. Erupting volcanoes provide natural disasters on a clockwork schedule; pirates' battles on the hour are staged in galleons on a man-made lagoon in the dry desert sand. While mom and dad "game," the children can meet Betty Boop and the Three Stooges in the Hollywood theme park—when they're not needed to hold their parents' buckets of quarters. The family that games together also shops together in the

3 ALAN HESS, *Viva Las Vegas, After-Hours Architecture* (San Francisco: Chronicle Books, 1993).

Forum Shops, a 250,000-square-foot addition to Caesar's World, where moving sidewalks take them through six triumphal arches rising from cascading fountains into the streets of stores. "Your typical Roman *via*," the critic Aaron Betsky reported on the occasion of the grand opening, "where the sun sets and rises on an electronically controlled cycle, continually bathing acres of faux finishes in rosy hues. Animatronic robots welcome you with a burst of lasers, and a Rococo version of the Fountain of the Four Rivers drowns out the sound of nearby slots." In Las Vegas "history repeats itself neither as farce nor as tragedy, but as a themed environment." [4]

"We come here a lot," said a couple from California who have made repeated visits with two small children; their only complaint was that they came too soon, in the pre-family-fun years. They'd have loved it even more, they explain, "if there was something else for the kids to do." Now, of course, Vegas has it all. But even with the expensive arcade games that the children played continually, this family found it a bargain next to a trip to Walt Disney World. A Nebraska family of five who stayed five days at Walt Disney World in January 1993 spent $4,445.21. It was not the high cost they objected to, however, or that the same money could buy a trip to a European city where real history and character are part of the package deal, along with architectural splendor, artistic treasures, and genuine culture and cuisine. Their only criticism of what few would call an authentic experience and some might call a self-inflicted hardship, was that that the government got $364.37 in taxes. [5]

Perhaps increasing competition will bring prices down, but it seems unlikely; Americans are more than willing to pay the freight. What they will get is more variety, and more competing themes. So apparent is the willingness to pay for erzatz experience that the idea of an amusement park based on the re-created Berlin Wall, complete with rides through Checkpoint Charlie, died only because no one was amused. How far can themed illusion go? To heavenly heights, if the theme park announced by the magician Doug Henning and the Maharishi Mahesh Yogi, spiritual advisor to the Beatles, ever materializes. [6] Their plan would turn 1,400 acres on the Canadian

4 AARON BETSKY, "Theme Wars Rage in Las Vegas," *Architectural Record*, August 1992, p. 29.

5 CATHY LYNN GROSSMAN, "Rising Fees Hit Tourists in the Wallet," *USA Today*, January 26, 1993.

6 "Veda Land: Theme Park for Ontario," *New York Times*, March 22, 1992.

side of Niagara Falls into Maharishi Veda Land, "a theme park combining recreation with spiritual enlightenment." There would be a Tower of World Peace, an International Summit Conference Center, a Heaven on Earth housing development (now there's an architectural challenge), and thirty-three rides and attractions reflecting the themes of enlightenment, knowledge, and entertainment. The rides would be designed by Hollywood special effects experts. With any luck and financing and those special effects, God could be alive and well in Veda Land. In the meantime, we had Heritage USA in South Carolina, Jim and Tammy Faye Bakker's "Christian retreat," where He was reputed to be doing well—until after the fall. Today, where else would one expect to find Him?

Once the substitute, or surrogate, is considered the more acceptable experience, remarkable things occur. There are rain forests in Las Vegas that casino guests find infinitely more impressive than the South American variety; they have seen the real thing on packaged tours but prefer the combination of tropicana and silks (the trade name for false foliage) with the added attraction of live white tigers. In Texas, when moviemakers planned a film about the Alamo and found the real landmark small and unprepossessing, they built a bigger and better Alamo in a nearby town. Today both the false and the genuine Alamo are equally popular tourist attractions. (If one is good, two are better. And the new, improved version is best of all.) A start has been made on taking the pressure off national parks by bringing tourists to a show-and-tell presentation of Zion Park livened up by advanced electronics, with a drive-by en route; one can experience it all this way and still get to Vegas that night.

Nor are the fine distinctions between the real fake and the fake fake always clear. It is easier to fake the unfamiliar than the better-known, and substitutes are more quickly accepted for what is not known at all. Only rarely does the result rise to the level where something new is invented out of the old. The surrogate version is usually a reduced and emptied-out idea based on what Corboz has called the "poverty of the re-invention of the not-known." But for those who dare to point out the depreciation of the product, or the discrepancies between the copy and the original, there are immediate charges of élitism or being the sorriest kind of spoiler, out of step with the temper and art of the times and the democratization that makes the substitute experience "available to everyone."

Surprisingly, it is only in the freewheeling commercial world that the substitute comes off. At a higher level, confusion is encouraged in a much more subtle and insidious and dangerous way, and the problem is far less intriguingly complex. In the world of art and scholarship, where they really know the difference, there is increasing confusion of real and fake, with a disturbing identification of the values of the original and the copy. The slippage is taking place at institutional and cultural sources that have always been the defenders and keepers of authenticity.

Museums, dependent on tourism, must compete for attendance with entertainment-geared attractions. To do that takes a lot of hype and high-class souvenirs in the gift shop. Museums of anthropology and natural history, in particular, have had to hustle to keep up with the appeal of reconstructions of native villages with computer-programmed figures performing rites and dances in full, reproduced regalia with hot-out-of-the-copy-shop accessories. The static displays of a history museum, no matter how impressive their actual artifacts, from the weathered Conestoga wagons that crossed plains and mountains to the battered pots and pans used on the long and dangerous westward trek, lose out to restored or re-created Old West saloons with shoot-outs on the hour. The real ghost towns disintegrate for lack of interest and funds.

The art, science, and culture museum of the University of California at Berkeley, located not in Berkeley but in the affluent suburb of Blackhawk, augmented its 1991 show of New Guinea artifacts with a "science theater," where an experience called Nature's Fury produced a rocking earthquake simulation from a minivolcano; going a step further for "lifelike" relevance appropriate to the community, a suggested survivor's kit was displayed in the trunk of a BMW. Life-size scenes in narrative settings increasingly subordinate the thing itself to a dramatic re-creation. With nothing to recommend them except their often shabby authenticity, the real objects simply have less appeal than snappy simulations.

While art museums are more removed from the tourist track where the "world's great masterpieces" are re-created in everything from living tableaux to glow-in-the-dark copies on velvet accompanied by unctious commentary and tangible awe, even the primary citadels have not escaped the trend. High art has been "contaminated"—Eco's word, no one else would dare use it—by the "blurring of the boundaries" of original and reproduction. It has become common practice for originals, reconstructions, and reproductions to be mingled in museum displays; one must read the exhibition labels to know what is real and what is not. But since few bother, the distinctions and their meaning are often lost. Nowhere else in the world is "the reconstructed datum already tainted by the original sin of the levelling of the pasts, the fusion of copy and original...the flattening of real against fake and the old on the modern," Eco reported, after a trip through the United States.[7]

This leveling of the works of art with the copies for sale in the museum shop is omnipresent. The ostensible purpose of the reproduction, to make one want the original, has been supplanted by the feeling that the original is no longer necessary. The copy is considered just as good and, in some cases, better; Eco and Baudrillard both argue that the simulation replaces the original to become the "reality"[8] in most minds, even if this is not overtly expressed, and even in those places meant to guard the uniqueness and the meaning of the work of art.

According to Margaret Crawford, an American studies specialist, and Richard Sennett, a sociologist and humanist who specializes in the philosophical and symbolic aspects of urbanism, there is a relationship between the museum shop and that feature of mall salesmanship called "adjacent attraction." In both the commercial and the cultural setting, there is a transfer of values from real objects of aesthetic and historical validity to lesser products. Even when direct copies are not involved, the frequent use of real objects as promotional devices raises the price and perception of the thing for sale, through the kind of association that "blurs the boundaries." But the process also works both ways. The commodity (for a price) becomes identified with qualities of the object (no price or, even, in the case of art works, priceless), so that the same value is given to both. As the "previously noncommodified entities become part of the marketplace...associations can resonate infinitely..."[9] and Eco's "flattening of values" sets in.

7 UMBERTO ECO, *Travels in Hyper Reality*, William Weaver, trans. (New York: Harcourt, Brace Jovanovich, 1986).

8 JEAN BAUDRILLARD, *Simulations*, Paul Foss, Paul Patton, and Philip Beitchman, trans. (New York: Semiotext(e), Inc., 1983).

9 MARGARET CRAWFORD, "The World in a Shopping Mall," in *Variations on a Theme Park*, Michael Sorkin, ed. (New York: Hill and Wang, 1992), 15.

Although they would be the last to actually promote it, museums do not actively discourage this perception. In fact, they have done much to encourage it through their increasing emphasis on the merchandise for sale in their ever expanding shops. The rationale seems to be that a well-made, mass-produced product that copies a one-of-a-kind work of art will increase appreciation of the uniqueness of the original; actually, the opposite seems to take place. Sales of manufactured copies of tomb-found ancient jewels and appealing reproduction sculptures are ringing up significant sales. They are judged qualitatively on the excellence of their copying techniques. Here we are in the terrible trap of "authentic reproduction" again. The well-made copy, virtually indistinguishable from the original (more mischief), meant to be enjoyed for its associations with the art object itself, ends up given the value of the object that inspired it, with all the meaningful differences smoothly eliminated. You can have your ancient Egyptian statue with the patina of time and the minor imperfections of use faithfully reproduced; it will actually be in much better shape than the fragile old piece with its freight of history, because it has been spared all those years in the tomb. The result is anything but benign. The copy corrupts the original because it has eliminated the sensibility triggered in part by the miracle of survival and the messages the object brings from the past—just those things that generate the response to the work of art. The substitute has falsely and misleadingly absorbed its values. The process is observable everywhere. "The principle of adjacent attraction is now operating at a societal level," Crawford informs us, "imposing an exchange of attributes between the museum and the shopping mall, between commerce and culture…history, technology, and art, as presented in the museums, have now become commodified."[10]

The museum visitor must run the gauntlet of these reproductions, never called copies since that word still has the scent of second-rateness, frequently even before seeing the original works of art. The Metropolitan Museum of Art in New York has inserted a multi-level, virtual small department store of reproduction, referential, and "related" merchandise just off the main lobby, where it can be entered without the museum's admission charge—sorry, "voluntary contribution" (never has the iron arm of euphemism worked so well), so that the visitor may come solely to buy without the expense and bother of entering the galleries at all. This is a common practice, since merchandising has become a major source of

10 CRAWFORD, op. cit., p. 30.

museum income or, at least, an essential supplement to fund-raising as costs escalate. (Annual reports show that the Metropolitan has also entered the modern world of leveraged development in the financing of its shop's construction; expansion with borrowed funds is the standard business wisdom brought to museum boards by their successful business directors. Profits are minimal while the payback takes place. What looks like a bonanza, isn't—at least not for a while. Curators' salaries, unleveraged, remain minimal.) Sales counters are often placed at both the entrances and exits to galleries or exhibitions. The quietly inescapable clack of the computer is the background music to all major shows.

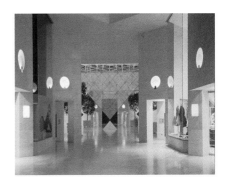

Crossing the line between high art and high-end merchandising at the Louvre in Paris: beyond I.M. Pei's museum concourse, a mall of designer boutiques, the Carrousel, "borrows" the upscale cultural ambience. *Photo courtesy of Pei, Cobb, Fried.*

Even Paris's princely Louvre has acknowledged the expectations of the museum-going public in its recent reconstruction. Beneath I. M. Pei's hotly debated glass pyramid in the Louvre's courtyard are the sales and social facilities expected today that were never envisioned in a royal palace. With typical panache and élan, the French have gone one step further in the dance with commerce. Along with the de rigueur museum shop, bookstore, and restaurant there is an underground shopping mall, a series of high-end "name" boutiques, like Chanel and Yves Saint-Laurent for the upscale tourist trade. No pandering, pussyfooting, or promotion here, just realistic recognition of a natural marketing opportunity with advantageous financial arrangements for all.

While art museums specialize in reproduction, other kinds of museums rely on reincarnation—stage-set displays of great moments in science or history, or reconstructions of settings in which actual artifacts may be displayed or activities or refreshments offered, efforts that range, in effect, from static to participatory theater. In natural history dioramas, long a favorite with the public and part of many children's early museum-visiting memories, the animals are real and the background artificial and illusionistic, often enhanced by real vegetable or mineral matter. We know this, of course; we are aware that the animals are stuffed and that we are being given a vicarious look at a reproduced habitat. New York's American Museum of Natural History has taken a commendable giant step toward clarification in its successfully reinstalled dinosaur halls: in most cases the real bones have been painstakingly reassembled, and where substitutes are used, the museum has gone to great pains to make the difference clear. This serves both education and authenticity. In most natural history museums, however, a trip to the aboriginal halls becomes riskier. Here the mingling of real and reproduced may be fudged for a livelier and more "realistic" representation of a strange world suggested by a combination of real and reproduced artifacts.

The blurring of boundaries has now become a constant in scholarship and connoisseurship. The computer increasingly substitutes the picture on the screen for the original work of art. Because the computer and the camera have made available an incredible array of research sources, arcane problems can be explored as never before; scholars are now able to deal with masses of data and remote collections of awe-inspiring completeness and diversity. This is one of the seductive miracles of the electronic age. Entire dissertations can be written without ever seeing the originals at all. Even when original documents and drawings are available, they are increasingly locked up and off-limits—particularly to students—for fear of deterioration; and when they can be used, they are seldom the major part of the study.

Since this is the point of scholarship where the eye is trained, and it is dealing with substitutes, the loss of direct experience is incalculable. It is through the immediate visual contact and primary sensory response engendered by repeated exposure to the actual work of art that connoisseurship is created—that related sequence of knowledge and taste by which works of art can be accurately understood, compared, defined, judged, and enjoyed. There is no replacement for this primary experience, no matter how technologically perfect the surrogate. The infinite, subtle cues and idiosyncratic signals of intent, finish, surface, and texture—the immediate contact with the hand of the artist in the actual touch of the pen or stroke of the brush —is paramount. When this relationship is dulled or diminished, the value placed on authenticity is diminished as well. Pedantic iconographic analysis is a poor replacement, particularly with the inevitable mistakes encouraged by the use of secondary sources.

One can, today, through superb photography, study details of the Sistine Chapel ceiling that are otherwise virtually impossible to see. But for something that can be held in the hand, in a variety of lights, or carefully restudied over a period of time—a drawing by a Renaissance master, for example, or a piece of sculpture—there is no replacement for the actual visual and tactile sensation; no matter how remarkably evocative and accurate the reproduction, it is still secondhand when impasto and pentimento simply become the slick computer screen. The perception and feel of the real thing involves a familiarity as close as the face of a loved one; as in a photograph, the expression becomes static as the remembered nuances fade. Computer communication is a tool, another surrogate for reality; it is useful documentation, not primary communication.

With authenticity increasingly devalued, and the copy considered an acceptable—even admirable—alternative, is it any wonder that there are "galleries" selling assembly-line Picassos complete with fraudulent signatures for ludicrous sums, and that they are being bought with full knowledge of their fakery?[11] Barnum was right, but there was more honesty, if one may insult the word, when the flimflam was pure and simple suckering of those too dumb or unfortunate to know the difference when the difference was still assumed to matter. What is appalling is that those who know enough not to want the fake Picassos still find it chic to argue that authenticity is no longer to be valued, that the imitation, in fact, has many advantages, such as availability and cost—which in this example, at least, seem to have gotten out of hand as the differences fade.

Eco of the impeccable, bemused, and outraged eye has given the subject an unexpected and very important spin. Rather than liking reality or the real thing too little, he says, Americans love it too much. We are obsessed with reality, with the possession of the object, determined to have it at any cost, in the most immediate and tangible form, unconcerned with authenticity or the loss of historical, cultural, or aesthetic meaning. This pervasive attitude, established through a massive popular network, has "spread to the products of high culture and the entertainment industry," Eco notes. The abrogation of values in the popularization of taste is near-universal; the relationship between value judgment and authenticity has virtually ceased to exist.

The theme park has no such problem of degenerative authenticity. Nothing in it is admired for its reality, only for the remarkable simulation that is achieved; the selective manipulation of its sources is a deliberate, expressive distortion that can be its own art form. It is not surprising that much of the most popular and profitable development of the genre is spearheaded and bankrolled by the masters of illusion; the movie and entertainment businesses have become the major innovators and investors in theme parks

11 WILLIAM H. HONAN, "Into an Age of Fake Art: A Very Real Quandary," *New York Times*, September 3, 1991.

and related enterprises. An entire new industry has grown up to serve themed entertainment, providing those erupting volcanoes and fiberglass rock formations on the grounds of Las Vegas casinos; according to an industry spokesman "you get a very artificial appearance with real rock." A California company called Wet Enterprise, which makes computerized fountains, developed much of the futuristic technology for EPCOT Center in Disney World. Those who wonder what happened to American know-how have just not been looking in the right places. This remarkable marriage of technologically based and shrewdly programmed artificial experience in a manufactured and managed environment, for a real-life substitute of controlled and pricey pleasures, is a totally American product.

With reality voided and illusion preferred, almost anything can have uncritical acceptance. Trendy exhibitions strip away everything of meaning or relevance for a perverse, camp reading that mutilates art and design history. "Interpretations" rush in to fill the vacuum where knowledge fails; research that retrieves reality is of less interest than critical inventions that subvert it. For those without memory, nostalgia fills the void. For those without reference points, novelties are enough. For those without the standards supplied by familiarity with the source, knock-offs will do. Escalating sensation supplants intellectual and aesthetic response. For all of the above, the outrageous is essential. There must be instant gratification; above all, one must be able to buy sensation and status; the experience and the products must be for sale.

Marketing Illusion

If the British are a nation of shopkeepers, Americans are a nation of shoppers. Whatever the Puritan ethic of frugality, parsimony, and guilt may have been, it is gone; the message on the T-shirt is Shop Till You Drop. Americans shop anywhere, buy anything. In every resort or theme park, behind every reconstructed facade, in every educational or entertainment venture, "related" merchandise is for sale. From the "credentialed" restoration, carried out by trained professionals, to the most blatant pit stop on marginal historic tours, there are shopping opportunities. Food, products, dreams, and desires are purveyed in settings designed to suggest everything from elegance to adventure.

On American highways, a fantasy landscape lures the speeding driver to eat and acquire. Tiki Villages stand next to Cathay Palaces, Leaning Towers of Pizza, Wild West Steak Houses, and the standardized expressions of assorted and exotic fast foods. Christmas Cottages offer seasonal make-believe all year. Trips to designer outlets that sell status goods off-price are a day's outing, a form of entertainment. One suspects that the images assembled and acquired are trophy bargains, seldom worn. Ye who travel the highway, abandon all time and place. Here is themed America for every pocketbook and taste.

In the interest of research, I spent one summer conscientiously sampling a classic American highway strip. Whatever the theme, the common culinary denominators were bland mediocrity and enormous portion size; one gets a lot of it, in a wide ersatz-ethnic range of menus and settings. In spite of the insistent stylistic static, nothing relieves the basic monotony. The idea of the grotesque in art and literature has traditionally been of something awesomely strange, unreal, and frightening; here the grotesque has become merely ludicrous—occasionally entertaining but more often reduced to total banality. This is a landscape that is flat and gross; it exists in response to the American automotive way of life. Its themed structures, many of them chains and franchises, are repeated endlessly and predictably. Anything truly outrageous would be welcome.

At the Hilltop Steak House in Saugus, a highway landmark near Boston celebrated for the enormous number of beef meals it serves with extraordinary dispatch, life-size plastic cows stand outside as cars whiz by. Patrons with numbered tickets in the hundreds queue up for rooms named Kansas City, Dodge City, Sioux City, and other

Theming it on the highway: a herd of life-size plastic cows makes it clear to the passing motorist that beef is the specialty at the Hilltop Steak House; a generic Oriental roof stands for generic Oriental food; a dry-docked roadside galleon beckons for fish. *Photos, Edward O. Nilsson.*

frontier figments of the gastronomic imagination. Not far away, a multiplex Oriental palace offers a variety of indistinguishable cuisines of cloyingly sweet-sauced sameness billed as Far Eastern in a selection of themed restaurants. Rivaling a hotel in the vastness of its lobbies and the number of its facilities, which have exhausted a mother lode of mass-produced black lacquer and pearl and equal amounts of plastic, it is clearly prepared to serve any function from birth to death. In a freewheeling eclecticism, fountains and bridges lead to booths with elaborately etched bistro-type glass partitions topped by a forest of Art Nouveau–type lamps. (Kublai Khan meets the hospitality industry.) Only the rest rooms remain resolutely utilitarian. Too bad, the missed opportunities tease the mind.

This imaging requires a certain attitude, as the word is currently used, an unabashed assurance combined with a limitless, undiscriminating innocence about the plundered sources, an imperviousness to the ridiculous, and absolutely no sense of irony. (Irony, S. J. Perelman once told us, is wasted on the Chinese—a statement so funny because it is so ludicrous, that today would be considered an ethnic slur and totally un-PC.) In fact, the more absurd the pretense and the place, the better; this is the new entrepreneurial given, simply the way things are done.

In the placelessness of suburbia and the strip, theming really counts. A shack in a parking lot can be a restaurant with battalions of stemware and menus as big as broadsides that imply cellar-stored wines and Lucullan feasts in flocked and gilded Styrofoam rococo splendor. That all this yields only the usual surf and turf, salad bar, and chocolate mud pie does not seem to disappoint. No one raised on Cinderella's Castle finds the place or the pretense incongruous. The building is always a darkened, windowless box, the illusion sealed against the surroundings; one stumbles out into the daylight and the waiting world of car washes and cut-rate minimalls.

Such surrealist destinations are the coordinates of suburban life. Considering the bland anonymity of these containers of products and services, which leapfrog the featureless landscape with its cloned office and shopping centers, the reliance on identification by association is not surprising.[1] Some of these places are not easy to

---

1 The apparent random isolation on fringe land is less haphazard than it seems; the location is usually selected to raise the local tax base and encourage new development.

forget. Anything can be invoked, given a sufficient stretch of imagination and a lack of fussiness about the result. Ignorance is the mother of invention, and the name of the land is Limbo.

Illusion is infinitely adaptable; what we see depends on who is doing the looking. John Cheever, writing in 1978 of the New England fast-food stands that resemble the House of Seven Gables or Colonial Williamsburg, believes that these images are "not picked for their charm or their claim to a past; [but] because we are a homeless people looking at nightfall for a window in which a lamp burns, and an interior warmed by an open fire, where we will be fed and understood and loved…" Cheever's reaction to the mix of fast food and fantasy has enormous pathos. He sees it as an escape from the solitary and mundane that marks so much of the present human condition. "The rash of utterly false mansards, false, small-paned windows, and electric candlesticks is the heart's cry of a lonely, lonely people," he writes.[2] Eco discerns another kind of emptiness in the rage for replicas. "A vacuum of memories," he calls it, "a present without depth."

The landmark as shopping mall: Faneuil Hall Marketplace, Boston, a uniquely American product, where "the successful packaging of authenticity" attracts almost as many visitors as Disneyland. *Photo courtesy of Faneuil Hall Marketplace.*

It is the union of culture and consumerism, however, that is a uniquely American phenomenon. The pre-Revolutionary enclave has its Colonial crafts-and-candle shop; the restored Western ghost town stocks penny candy and quaint merchandise in its general store. But perhaps the most notable American marketing invention is the festival marketplace, where merchandising is married to preservation for shopping as entertainment in a historical architectural setting. Buildings of genuine antiquity, such as Boston's superb 1820s Greek Revival Quincy Market, are restored and turned into upscale shopping centers. Where suitable structures are lacking, carefully themed new construction is built to take advantage of the ambience, as on Baltimore's waterfront.

These places have an enormous appeal. It is not without significance that at one time an equal number of people visited Boston's Faneuil Hall Marketplace and Disneyland, nor should it be surprising that shopping has become the end of the preservation rainbow. But it takes constant vigilance to retain the special character of these places, while holding off their homogenization and reduction to a common, familiar level of standard chain stores and tourist trivia. Even the Faneuil Hall Marketplace, an exemplary demonstration of

2 John Cheever, *The Journals of John Cheever* (New York: Knopf, 1981), 346.

the marriage of commerce and history at the start, has now been malled, with an appalling loss of identity and integrity.

The father of the festival marketplace, the developer James W. Rouse, blazed a trail for what Margaret Crawford has called the "successful packaging of 'authenticity.'"[3] Rouse shrewdly understood that genuine architecture, with its rich associative details, ameliorated (to use the popular buzzword that excuses the inexcusable) the usual synthetic and bland nature of the standard shopping mall. Its unique features and residual legitimacy provide color and interest. It would be unfair to ignore the fact that Rouse's enterprises have saved landmarks and raised consciousness about an endangered heritage; many buildings that would have been lost are still standing due to his entrepreneurial vision. His example offered a viable and attractive alternative to demolition, and others have followed his lead with varying degrees of fidelity and success. Daniel H. Burnham's magnificent Union Station in Washington, D.C., after many years of marginal survival (a huge hole in the ground left from an aborted preservation attempt was eventually filled with a visitors' center that failed), has had a spectacular commercial reincarnation on the Rouse model. The building's extraordinary monumental architecture upgrades the shopping experience far beyond its customary characterless container.

But the formula has had some deeply disturbing fallout. Crawford has noted the negative aspects of the use of authenticity as a sales tool. An appropriation of values takes place in which the merchandise borrows an aura of quality and authenticity from the source or setting. This is a process that Crawford and others call the "commodification" of American culture. In this increasingly common phenomenon, the authentic, noncommercial commodity —objects, activities, or images—becomes commodified indirectly through absorption into the commercial setting where everything else is for sale.[4] There is a transfer of the values of the genuine article —the singular ambience, or the art or antiquities used as promotional display—to the ordinary objects being sold. This confuses and ultimately cheapens what is authentic, through a subtle and pervasive process of identification that gives equal value to both. Through this loss of definition and blurring of differentiation, the

3 MARGARET CRAWFORD, "The World in a Shopping Mall," in *Variations on a Theme Park*, Michael Sorkin, ed. (New York: Hill and Wang, 1992). 3–30.

4 Ibid., 14–17.

inauthentic takes on an air of authenticity. In the festival market-place, the unusual qualities of the historical setting are tranferred to ordinary merchandise that is often the trendy duplicate of that found in most commercial malls, giving it a special gloss and synthetic value by suggestive association.

There is also the less remarked but pervasive mutilation by salva-tion of the less accomodating historic landmarks. Burnham's Beaux Arts train station, with its heroic statues ringing an immense coffered, vaulted ceiling, or the rows of continuous Greek Revival brick-and-granite Boston market buildings by Alexander Parris, are so strong and beautiful that they dominate the familiar and redundant mix of merchandise. Other survivals are not so fortunate. When the historical fabric is fragile or discontinuous, as at New York's South Street Seaport, authenticity is lost or compromised by forcing it into the merchandising mold; most of the eccentric, believable, and vulnerable remains are sacrificed to the clichés of commercial gentrification, distorted and vulgarized by the marketing formulas. The architecture itself is commodified. And while the genuine historical fragment is a plus, it is not really considered necessary; it can be replicated or suggested in a themed environment that creates a simulacrum of authenticity, or a pastiche of signals and references that will do just as well.

With its up-front emphasis on consumerism as social life and enter-tainment, as wish- and dream-fulfillment, the shopping center is the consummately American-made place. Shopping, American style, was simply a place waiting to happen; someone had to invent it. One of the inventors was Addison Mizner, creator of the palm-shaded and flower- and shop-filled "vias" of the 1920s that turn Worth Avenue in Palm Beach into an extravagant fairy tale. Everyone can be Cinderella or the Prince. From this small and elegant beginning, the shopping center's development—as fantasy, as derived experience, as themed environment—is an explosive story. Even the early, strictly functional, postwar shopping centers of the 1950s and 1960s, open to the elements, "anchored" by two department stores, seem to belong to some commercial Stone Age.

Today, the mall (think about that word and image—I wonder who first invoked it) consists of multiple air-conditioned atriums (think about that word, too) linking an endless maze of indoor shopping allées (more preemptive linguistics) punctuated by repeated fast-food "courts." There is an equally endless feeling of déjà vu. Blaming the monotony on modernism, the reductive boxes have acquired "architecture." Potemkin villages offer postmodernist facades with false dormers, towers, arches, windows, and trim in shades of mauve, pumpkin, and pistachio; these "buildings" are manipulated into simulated streets and squares that go nowhere except to more of the same. They are not meant to convince; they simply supply a background architectural identity; in fashion it is known as a look.

San Diego's Horton Plaza (1985), by the acknowledged master of the genre, Jon Jerde, is a pastel pseudo-vernacular "urban" experience on the street; inside, it combines equal parts of stagecraft and sales wizardry. Jerde's more developed models excerpt the city's "themes" by appropriating the "essence" of its neighborhoods to serve as settings for the shops and restaurants. He calls this "retrofitting suburban and obsolete urban environments, creating people places which are significantly signatured to the host community's unique reality." In with significantly signatured reality. Out with real reality—particularly those unappealing aspects of real city life. The city as "host" provides the signals, but some very strange signals are being given. The extracted and exploited token place as marketing gimmick is preferred by many to the less convenient, safe, or sanitary city itself. No one ever needs to experience that unique reality at all, and there are, in fact, generations for whom the mall is the substitute urban experience. Thus the ultimate absurdity is achieved: an edited and appropriated version of exactly those distinguishing, organic features of a city that characterize it, reduced to a merchandising theme — the city as sales promotion.

Jerde has coined the phrase "experiential placemaking" for his work, a concept that reached full flower in Japan with the opening of Canal City Hakata Fukuoka, in April 1996. Experiential placemaking, he explains, is the "fabrication of rich, experiential places which… inspire and engage the human spirit"[5] while "combatting the decline of twentieth-century cities…by formulating a new vision of the city and town center." This "third millennium city," as he has named and promoted it, is "an environmental loom through which the whole polychromatic cloth of a restored *corpus civitatis* is celebrated, a loom enfolding nature and humankind in an ongoing partnership through which the unknown evolutionary potentials of each are realized." The commercial center goes cosmic.

5 All quotations on Jerde projects are taken from promotional material from the Jerde office.

After the suburban megamall, the fusion of commerce and entertainment in the city: Canal City Hakata, Fukuoka, Japan, is mallmaster Jon Jerde's polychrome vision of the new town center that has it all. *Photos courtesy of the Jerde Partnership.*

The loom woven in Japan is modestly billed as a "walk through the universe." Five zones are built around a canal, incorporating "the stars, moon, sun, earth and sea"; there are areas designated as a Moon Walk, Earth Walk and Sea Court, as well as the more conventional mix of theater, cinemas, department stores, hotels, and offices. Canal City is polychromatic, all right; its broadly color-banded buildings reach a fevered pitch of flamboyant hyperbole. Stylistically, it might best be characterized as short-attention-span architecture. The architect refers to his source as the striated rock formations of the nearby river. A more down-to-earth characterization of the project describes it as a response to "market-driven demand" and "a strong value creator for contemporary real estate development." Experiential placemaking may work for Fukuoka and troubled towns already decimated by the flight of business to malls and edge developments, but for most communities significantly signatured reality sounds more like a city-buster than salvation. As a way to create a "fundamentally new expression of city" it is a stunning exercise in architectural and urban hubris. There is an awful lot of moondust in the mix.

The first time I noticed the opportunistic and self-delusory nature of exploited identity (there is nothing credible or innocent about this calculated cannibalism, although a certain monumental wrong-headedness and insensitivity are involved) was when I visited the new shopping center built to fill the vast hole in the heart of Paris where the traditional and irreplaceable food market, Les Halles, formerly stood. The great iron-and-glass sheds and the sights, sounds, and tastes of the "belly of Paris" had been replaced by a fluorescent underground maze of identical, eventless corridors connecting repeated shops; the same boutiques kept reappearing in the same uninflected glare. Signs bearing the names of the old streets that had been demolished above ground marked the underground corridors in a gesture of total, mocking irrelevance. In the language of the streets, Paris had been dissed.

The apogee of the appropriated genre may be a superb bit of sophistry tucked artfully behind Beverly Hills's glittering Rodeo Drive. As impressive as it is improbable, this cunningly curved new shopping street with its evocative mix of quasi-Continental prototypes is extremely well done; it is most effective as a classy showcase for high-end luxury goods. The expert appropriation of the hallmarks of historical European examples in the form of tiny John Nash terraces and miniature Beaux Arts mansions turns postmodern cuteness to serious upmarket classical. It is like a really good Hollywood set—you might call it the Merchant-Ivory mini-mall version, impeccably detailed. The sophisticated execution is the ultimate demonstration of the use of history, real or invented, as a marketing ploy. This is commodified architecture *sans pareil*. What is disturbing is not so much the thing itself, however, which bases its appeal on its very artificiality, as the carryover of its "lessons" to buildings and areas where the remnants of an indigenous and legitimate urbanity created by culture and custom are being replaced by merchandising make-believe.

As surely as superhighways lead to parking lots, the shopping center and the theme park had to meet. Their marriage, made in corporate heaven, created the megamall, with the theme park at its heart. Curiously, the first megamall appeared in Canada, where exported American culture has always been suspect. Alberta's West Edmonton Mall, opened in 1986, covered 5.2 million square feet and was proudly advertised as being larger than a hundred football fields; it held (briefly) several Guinness world records for the size of its indoor amusement park, water park, and parking lot. To its "Parisian boulevards," lined with shops, department stores, restaurants, and movie theaters were added a nightclub and a chapel. (We are getting close to a life-to-death experience; schools and clinics have been featured in later examples, but as of this writing, there are no mortuaries.) Its own Fantasyland Hotel, with themed international rooms—echoes of that California pop-cult icon, the Madonna Inn in San Luis Obispo—is advertised with the promotional lure, "What country do you want to sleep in tonight?"

Here was fantasy run amok—and all downhill. Crawford's vivid description of the wem, as it was quickly called, suggests creative chaos: "a replica of Columbus's *Santa Maria* floats in an artificial lagoon, where real submarines move through an impossible seascape of imported coral and plastic seaweed inhabited by live penguins and electronically controlled rubber sharks; fiberglass columns crumble in simulated decay beneath a spanking new Victorian iron bridge;…fake waves, real Siberian tigers, Ching-dynasty vases, and mechanical jazz bands are juxtaposed in an endless sequence of skylit courts…. Confusion proliferates at every level; past and future collapse meaninglessly into the present; barriers between real and fake, near and far, dissolve as history, nature, technology, are indifferently processed by the mall's fantasy

"More" is more of the same at the Mall of America, where redundant atriums repeat the standardized chains in universal mallstyle. *Photo courtesy of the Jerde Partnership.*

machine."[6] It was West Edmonton's hubris (or its developers'), and its chief claim and selling point, that the entire world existed within its walls. Actually, as one discovered, it existed several times over. The formula, however, is the same blend of standard real estate, financing, and marketing practices perfected over several decades of mall investment. As Crawford points out, this was simply an elephantine version of the regional shopping center, offering more outrageous claims and outlandish features.

Inevitably, America took back its own. The Mall of America, outside Minneapolis, designed by Jon Jerde, has it all on an even larger scale—plus office towers, several hotels, and a conference center. Conference centers attract still more people, which generates more hotel business and more merchandise and entertainment sales. (Obviously, the title of biggest is never going to stick; like the tallest skyscraper, there will always be a new one that holds the championship fleetingly.) What is much more significant than its size is the fact that it was at the Mall of America that the shopping center and the theme park formed their triumphant and permanent alliance. The centerpiece is a Knott's Berry Farm theme park, Camp Snoopy, set into a landscape made to resemble the northern Minnesota countryside for verisimilitude. Snoopy and other characters greet visitors "live." Mickey, meet Snoopy. Only Snoopy never sleeps: Mall of America, like the WEM, is a twenty-four-hour operation.

"Our idea is to create a complete city with complex fragments," Jerde has explained. This city has no "evident architecture"; it is entered through department stores and parking lots. Inside are "quintessential streets and districts…very hip zones, traditional all-American zones, garden zones, and so on. Each place within the mall will reflect a theme."[7] An indoor mall that Jerde proposed for New York presented themed areas inspired by different parts of the city: Madison Avenue for yuppies, Fifth Avenue for the very rich, Third Avenue for evening entertainment, "Canal Street for surplus," with each area "a concentration of retail designed to attract a specific type of shopper."[8] It takes a special point of view to reduce New York to such calculated, stereotypical absurdity, to believe that a successful substitute for the city's vagaries and

6 CRAWFORD, op. cit., 3–4.

7 JOHN JERDE, "Instant City," *Arch+*, nos. 114–115 (December 1992), 117.

8 Ibid.

indecencies has been devised. It will have been purged of its undesirable (and unmarketable) features, such as its impure cosmopolitan and stylistic mix, lively and sometimes sordid incongruities, real or imaginary dangers, and earthy urban overlay. New Yorkers, notoriously and irascibly fond of their city, may not find this as enchanting an idea as Californians, who have already embraced a mall version of appropriated Los Angeles neighborhoods. No mall could begin to reproduce the sophisticated variety and international glamour of Madison Avenue, or the unanticipated and intriguing preciosity of the transformed SoHo, where restored, ornate nineteenth-century industrial architecture houses a high-style, avant-garde consumer culture of art galleries and individually conceived and owned shops. The marvels of modern merchandising leave me cold when measured against this miraculous mix of urban accretions and survivals. You can design Utopia, and many have tried and failed. No one, from Tony Garnier to Patrick Geddes, knew that shopping would be the glue to hold it together.

In New York's SoHo, owner-operated shops and restaurants, experimental art galleries, and converted lofts fill the handsomely adapted industrial structures of the city's nineteenth-century cast-iron district, a setting that even the invading chains cannot destroy. The unexpected or unusual is the norm. *Photos, Caroline Kane and Laura T. George.*

Like the theme park phenomenon, the malling of America has been commented on by the mile. What has generally escaped attention, however, is the managed nature of its product and clientele or, to put it more melodramatically, the co-opting of the consumer, willingly co-opted though he or she may be. The American shopping center is not, as commonly believed, an indigenous, spontaneous expression of instinctive or intuitive cultural and consumer patterns, something as American as the flag, as natural and inevitable as free choice and free enterprise can make it. In the American belief system, there are things you simply don't fool around with. It is, of course, a one-sided con game, in which the investor, not the consumer, always wins. There are no real choices, either those of natural selection or of a free market. Both concept and design are calculated elements in a skillful and strategic marketing plan, specifically targeted and carefully replicated. Whether the complex takes the form of a converted landmark or glitzy new construction, the underlying principle is the same. Whatever the style, the result is rigidly and exclusionistically shaped by a carefully devised formula based on the essential kind and number of shops—department store anchors, specialty retail and restaurant chains—considered necessary for an established level of merchandising profit. In every case, success or failure is measured strictly in terms of dollars per square foot.

Crawford is a particularly penetrating scholar of the phenomenon; she gives an illuminating, detailed account of the remarkable techniques and strategies involved.[9] She explains how the real estate, financing, and marketing expertise and the scale of investment required have limited the field to large developers with major resources, virtually eliminating competition. Established patterns are repeated rigidly and uniformly; no one tinkers with what works. The look, quality level, and general ambience are determined by meticulously researched consumer profiles that go beyond income analysis and buying habits to "psychographics," which identify "aspirations as well as needs...'identity' as well as income."[10] This, in turn, sets the nature of the stores, their merchandise and mix, number and location. The deadly sameness that marks these places is absolutely intentional. This fine-tuned calculation is repeated for similar areas, subject to adjustment as needed. Restrictive clauses in leases set and maintain guidelines that specify everything from design to prices. This standardization of setting and goods is meant to guarantee a meticulously conceived and predictable profit formula and cash flow, as much as the better-publicized aim of acceptable uses and atmosphere.

That these places fill many needs engendered by the patterns of commercial residential development is a truism. Moreover, American enterprise will continue to find new ways to meet and exploit those needs. The rise of the superstore, literally covering acres with discount and specialized merchandise—the Wal-Marts, Home Depots, and warehouse-type supermarkets (the "box" stores) —has almost superseded the mall for serious shopping; it can be located on the highway or in isolation where land is cheap and available. The mall now comes closer to its implications of casual entertainment, somewhere to stroll and seek amusement, a place for impulse buying. Teenagers, hanging out, have always used it this way. It has even become the place to exercise for the elderly, who meet and walk before the stores are open.

But the more one experiences the "mall miracle," and the more it replaces the downtowns and small communities that it destroys and

9 CRAWFORD, op. cit., 6-11.

10 "Indexes such as VALS (the Values and Life Styles program), produced by the Stanford Research Institute, correlate objective measures, such as age, income, and family composition with subjective indicators such as value systems, leisure preferences, and cultural backgrounds to analyze trade areas."

makes obsolete, becoming progressively and increasingly shabby and empty, the clearer it becomes that something crucial and vital is missing. What is not so clear to the consuming public is that this something is exactly what has been deliberately eliminated from all of the calculations by those who control them. There has been little awareness, and less scrutiny, of the kind of controls exercised and what has been deliberately eliminated or lost.[11]

Why bother about Big Brother when we can be manipulated by our own needs and greed? There is none of the traditional kind of competition that leads to the innovation, invention, and experimentation that have been a unique and characteristic feature of American entrepreneurship; in fact, this is actively discouraged as unpredictable and risky. What has been sacrificed to the certainty of the reliable, preset formula is variety, serendipity, and spontaneity. What is outlawed is originality and nonconforming, creative design and marketing. What is gone are options—those qualities of chance, the unusual, the unpredictable, the offbeat—and the constant revisions that have always given cities their renewable, changing, variable, cosmopolitan, living character. There are no mavericks, no hot young designers, no individualized products or styles, no start-ups or successes, nothing unexpected or unusual, nothing to surprise or delight, no opportunity for anything to be nurtured or to grow, no creative energy, no new or unconventional ideas. In no way does this controlled set of enterprises supply the interest, excitement, and products for which the city is the traditional incubator.

Whatever the level, from high-end to off-price, this is a homogenized mass-market culture of only the most highly promoted, massively invested in, widely distributed, standardized style and entertainment—the most uniform, market-proven fashion and products. In the ever expanding mall culture, around the corner just

11 After reading Crawford's analysis, I understood why negotiations in New York between the Rouse Company and the South Street Seaport had deadlocked on which blocks preservationists thought were best to save and convert for commercial use, and whether or not connecting new construction would compromise them. It was all a matter of arithmetic—by Rouse's calculations, the buildings had to be accommodated to a specified number of continuous, uninterrupted "shopping" feet, rather than the other way around, and no deviation was possible. There was also an attempt to put in trees and decorative paving as in other "festival marketplaces," but New Yorkers, clinging to their authentic, historic waterfront grunginess, resisted.

means more of the same. The sameness comes in two standard styles: numbingly ordinary or conventionally classy. The fountain-filled atriums of pricey upscale boutiques and the jerry-built, plain-pipe discount stores are unvaryingly, and often literally, identical. There are the same "international" food courts, with the same plastic-packaged, franchised, ethnic fast food in familiar "signal" colors and fluorescent settings. Even the expensive boutiques are chains, safely and identifiably replicated—Tiffany and Rodier at the top of the scale, K Mart and J C Penney farther down. The only change is a constant weeding out and replacing for sustained prof-itability and uniformity. The individual retailer is discouraged with less favorable terms and shorter leases than the national chains. Each entity operates according to a set of inclusionary and exclusionary practices determined by management policies.

It works, of course; only the consumer is being shortchanged. There is no way to believe that this is all, and everything America wants, when entrepreneurship becomes a function of land values, lending practices, leveraged real estate development, and conglomerate corporate ownership looking to the enormous bottom line. It is not enough to suggest that this is the course of true capitalism, like true empire (an idea that has long since lost currency or meaning). The rules and the profits must be reliable and reasonably risk-free for the investors who have replaced the traditional independent entrepreneurs. The stake is now the whole, often huge, complex; the overriding interest and root of the matter are the real estate.

It is these policies that determine the ever escalating but unvarying experience; it is these formulas that will never permit anything different or better. Millions of teenagers may wish to wallow in the same crop tops and jeans; this does not mean that there is no market for other designs or original ideas. No matter how numerous the courts, or how soaring the atriums, or how endless the repetitive vistas, the restrictive unreality and narrow range of experience come through ultimately as a soporific bore. Climate-controlled and timeless, except for the switch in the seasonal departments from outdoor furniture to Christmas decorations, the mall is a uniquely affectless and ambiguous environment. We have many accounts of the disorientation and anomie of the addicted user—from William Kowinski's *mal de mall* and Joan Didion's "state of aqueous suspen-sion" to something known as the "Gruen Transfer," from pioneer mall architect Victor Gruen's definition of the point at which the visitor with a product and purpose in mind—the "destination buyer"—loses it to become an impulse shopper.[12]

In the reality of suburban America, of course, there is no place else to go. The movies are also in the mall, since movies and shopping are the two great American pastimes. We are avid moviegoers, compulsive escapees, vicarious viewers of the endless and marvelous possibilities of other lives and places. Simulation provides it all. It is the cinema that gives us the variety of experience and environment that a mall and theme park culture denies us; it is the movies that supply, secondhand, a range of images more beautiful or ugly, serene or violent, imaginative and complex, filtered through art, than can be experienced in suburban subdivisions and shopping centers. But in the world of simulation, everything doubles back on itself. The fastest-growing theme park is the re-created movie set or back lot, where the visitor imagines himself an actor in the story on a re-created setting that is a copy of an earlier, unreal place.

Perhaps substitute experience has lulled our desire for genuine diversity; we accept not only controlled products of assured uniformity but the controlled environment as well. The changeover from the street to the enclosed, security-controlled mall, where one feels safer than on city streets and where so much of our social and communal life has been relocated, has transformed and diminished the use and meaning of the public domain. There is a growing controversy as to whether the mall is public or private space, with constitutional freedoms or its own police powers. The critic Michael Sorkin argues that this murky area—the increasing privatization of publicly used malls as a substitute for the almost extinct communal function of the street and the square—marks a trend toward the end of public space, with alarming ramifications in terms of democratic diversity and freedoms.[13] Court cases increasingly test freedom of speech and assembly issues in these privately owned, controlled, and administered environments. The cocoon of the mall protects not only from assorted discomforts but also from diversity. The conforming comforts of this consumer culture, with the instant gratification of its predictable places and pleasures, is the underpinning of the unreal America.

12 CRAWFORD, op. cit., p.14.

13 *Variations on a Theme Park*. Michael Sorkin, ed. (New York, Hill and Wang, 1992), xi–xv.

Illusion and Architecture

previous pages: Architecture as illusion and allegory: John Hejduk, The Thirteen Watchtowers of Cannaregio.

How does architecture operate in the unreal America? With difficulty and with compromise. Architecture is deeply affected by the reality of client, economics, and taste. While architects must always function within the norms and practices of a society in order to practice at all, the ground rules have changed so radically, and the context is so altered, that both the art and the profession face unusual problems and challenges. Architecture exists within a culture that assigns the priorities and values that control all of its decisions.

Never has this culture been so much a function of investment economics, or have those investment strategies been practiced on such a gargantuan scale. The architect's choice is to join the system or lose the commissions and the visibility essential to his existence, both of which are tied to the high-risk stakes and high profit margins of real estate and the entertainment industry. Architecture will survive as an art; it always has. But one can no longer say that the artist struggles but prevails, that great art will always beat the system and rise to its proper level. The odds against this are formidable today.

Moreover, the connection between architecture and the profitable popular culture raises questions that reverberate throughout our society. How and what we build encapsulates the life of an age; what we believe in and what matters to us are clearly revealed in everything from the meanest to the most monumental structure. My purpose has been to suggest how pervasively this popular culture has affected us and our architecture in ways and on levels of which we are not aware, through the evolution and manipulation of taste and desire and, ultimately, as an economic rather than an aesthetic phenomenon.

The relationship between imitation and authenticity is fluid, perverse, and unclear, and any attempt to sort it out or set it right is, in itself, unreal and doomed from the start. To find this relationship less than wonderful, however, does not indicate dismissal or require blind reformist zeal; that would be unreal and arrogant as well. It is a fascinating phenomenon, with twists and turns that astonish, appall, and amuse; the exchange of meanings and flattening of differences between real and unreal produces mind-blowing hybrids and awesome junk with equal ease. Miles Orvell has pointed out that authenticity as an essential element of art and culture was embraced only in the twentieth century, as a reaction against the increasingly debased and derivative eclecticism of the machine-produced copies of the arts that the nineteenth century loved. This "culture of authenticity" became the bedrock of modernism.[1] But the desire for easily made and ever-improving replicas has continued into the twentieth century as mainstream popular taste and, ultimately, as a badge of correct taste. In an ironic switch, the factitious is no longer compared to the original but has become its own thing, accepted as the thing itself and considered equal or better.

The modern movement saw the machine not as a purveyor of replicas but as having its own intrinsic production aesthetic of simplicity and rationality, where form was based on utilitarian logic and manufacturing methods. Thus understood, the argument went, the machine would not only better serve art and society but would also save the world from secondhand kitsch. It was no contest; kitsch won, hands down. Today, taste rides a roller coaster of popular vernacular and esoteric avant-garde. High culture borrows from low, changing low art into high art in the process, as in Claes Oldenburg's soft sculptures of hamburgers and monumental baseball bats and clothespins, which imbued those banal objects with wit and cultural gravity, with reverberating meanings that turned them into icons of our time. The more adventurous culturati have embraced the awesome "originals" of streamlined diners and drive-ins and the archetypal kitsch of pink flamingos, attracted by the offbeat pleasures of camp and the nostalgia of the cultural near-past. Thus we have a circular aesthetic, with intriguing inversions of meaning and value.

But while high taste and low taste have been consummating their union, a great divide has opened between what is most serious and what is most popular in the arts. In architecture, there is a growing chasm between architects and their clients, between professionals and public, a distancing of buildings and their users, a widening gap between an increasingly complex and hermetic art and a product designed for instant appeal and quick commercial success. Into this gap has come escape architecture—the user-friendly substitutes, the buildings-in-costume, and the pretend-places favored by preservationists, builders, investors, and the consuming public. Postmodernism has been a kind of revenge on modernism among philistines and intellectuals alike, a comforting justification

---

1 MILES ORVELL, *The Real Thing: Imitation and Authenticity in American Culture, 1880–1940* (Chapel Hill: University of North Carolina Press, 1989).

for a public that had stubbornly resisted both the modernist aesthetic and morality. One can see why decorative recall is easier to like than the more demanding structures that enlarge the definition and experience of architecture and advance the building art. The familiar, the undemanding, and the unambiguous exert an understandable attraction; disturbing responses to problematic conditions have little appeal. Precisely what is most remarkable about the new architecture—the subtle and searching complexities that seek to break through existing conventions, its often radical or recondite nature—makes it most vulnerable to the merchants of high-end schlock. And for those merchandisers who have found architecture to be one more marketable product, these buildings are a hard sell.

The fact is that this is not easy architecture for the public, and architecture has always been a public art. It lacks instant appeal; it does not yield its virtues readily. It has no common public language, as in the past. Until this century the public and the profession shared a known vocabulary; the divide between them was simply a matter of the degree to which traditional forms were mutually understood. Like so much else in the arts, architecture has taken new forms and developed a new and often arcane vocabulary. The alienation that started with the distrust and dislike of the unfamiliar in modern architecture has been exacerbated by the increasingly abstract and esoteric nature of current philosophy and practice. What has taken place is a near-total divorce of the best new work from a public that barely understands it and cares less, that no longer sees it as central to a society's image and spirit—and, in fact, hardly sees it at all.

It is not surprising, then, that government policy promotes cheapness and expediency as politically correct, that architecture is seen as a frill to be avoided as a virtuous protection of the taxpayers' money. Names like Frank Lloyd Wright and Philip Johnson may be recognized and even respectfully regarded, but this has to do more with personality and celebrity than with art. A public preoccupied as never before with fantasy, hooked on simulation, and satisfied with surrogate experience made possible by unprecedented advances in technology, is neither aware of nor interested in real architecture. There has been a singular loss of communication between the real world and the synthetic world; the art closest to us and our lives has become particularly remote.

Many architects, enthusiastically or through a process of rationalization, have simply joined the biggest game going, in a variety of ways, part-time or full-time, for better and for worse. They have seized the opportunity to jump on a bandwagon that would make them both avant-garde and available. Arguments and styles have been devised to serve the new muses of fantasy, nostalgia, and camp, heavily weighed down (although the product is essentially light-weight) with the transferred freight of symbolism, metaphor, and narrative adapted from linguistic and philosophical studies in vogue. With the recognition and celebration of the pop landscape, it has been possible to loosen and expand the boundaries of accepted taste and practice. Although Eco is one of the leading linguistic scholars whose influence is frequently cited, he condemns what he calls a "contaminated culture." He does not see it as something stemming from high philosophical sources but believes that it derives directly from the widely disseminated, already degraded products of the entertainment industry. The big names—the "signature architects" (a term invented by developers) of those builders who find that architectural celebrities can be sold as status symbols like any other designer item—are employed directly by the Disney fantasy factory and the largest commercial interests; the rest work for business or commercial clients as they always have, offering market versions of make-believe or ameliorating, when permitted, the kind of schmaltzy bricolage favored by most builders and their buyers.

Michael Eisner, CEO of the Walt Disney Company, has employed some of the world's best-publicized practitioners for the multi-plying hotels, shopping facilities, and office buildings that serve the Disney empire. But, ultimately, the planners and image makers are not the architects; the same sticky style that overlays it all comes from the "imagineers." The architects supply creativity and credibility for Disney's strictly enforced guidelines, budgets, and basic design concepts. A EuroDisney opening-day newspaper photograph showed Robert A. M. Stern, Michael Graves, and Frank Gehry, three of Eisner's architectural Mouseketeers, in front of a Gehry-designed minimall. Only Gehry says, regretfully, "I lost control." In California and Florida, Graves has mastered the Disney genre with several structures that include a headquarters building where the Seven Dwarfs support a classical pediment, amid other droll grotesqueries, as well as themed Swan and Dolphin hotels. Stern, who sits on the Disney board, has had a successful career based largely on his role as a kind of Ralph Lauren of architecture;

The Disneyfication of architecture: *top,* Team Disney Building, Burbank, California, by Michael Graves, with the Seven Dwarfs as nineteen-foot-tall caryatids supporting the building's pediment. *Disney characters* © Disney Enterprises, Inc. *Used by permission from Disney Enterprises, Inc. Photo by Jeff Goldberg/Esto.*

The Swan (or Dolphin) hotel, Disney World, Orlando, Florida, by Michael Graves, *middle,* where anthropomorphic fantasy keeps the magic alive. *Photo by Jeff Goldberg/Esto.*

bottom, Newport Bay Club Hotel, Disneyland, France, by Robert A. M. Stern, extending and exporting the fantasy in mock New England shingle style. *Disney characters* © *Disney Enterprises, Inc. Used by permission from Disney Enterprises, Inc.*

he has perfect pitch for the details that create the images that unite memories and aspirations in a mix of status symbols and consumer comforts. Eisner has a star-studded lineup. One wonders, though, who is having whom. There is no denying the expertise of the artifice, the planning and organization, the innovative technology, the masterful marketing, and the assured understanding of popular tastes and pleasure. But then is something witlessly opportunistic about those architects who, following their jubilant discovery of suburbia and the short-order construction of the highway strip, have adopted the theme park and its cartoon characters as their latest Holy Grail.

Can the architect draw his motifs and messages from a contaminated culture without danger? Does our delight in the deadpan outrageousness of some of the more spontaneous manifestations of popular taste lead to much more than a trendy dead end? Will the act of appropriation, engaged in by selective and sophisticated sensibilities, create anything better than a marginal product? Is this incorporation a truly creative procedure or a patronizing, elitist act? Do we co-opt these popular objects and images, or are we co-opted by them? Finally, does the debasement of the borrowed idea or fabric taken from high art corrupt high art as well, as Eco suggests? Are we producing still another kind of art and reality—or simply speeding the degenerative process?

I part company with those who see the popular culture as the source of cosmic lessons about architecture and design. Obviously, some useful things are to be learned and appropriately applied; there is even an occasional epiphany for the intellectual elite when they discover what today's world is all about. And while I love quirky drive-ins and Googie survivals,[2] the fun lasts just about as long as the Dairy Freeze; still, I infinitely prefer these offbeat and idiosyncratic expressions of the consumer culture to the standardized commercialism of the fast-food mediocrity that stretches from sea to shining sea.

I am not one of those who deny or wish away the environmental realities of our day. The highway and the commercial strip, the suburb and the shopping mall are there because they fill needs, and whether those needs could be filled in different or better ways is

2 Alan Hess, *Googie: Fifties Coffee Shop Architecture* (San Francisco: Chronicle Books, 1985).

moot. But to suggest that strip malls and shopping centers offer anything more than the most limited applications to an art far richer in its sources, infinitely more complex in its purposes, and so much larger in its reach, is an act not of inspiration but of impoverishment. I do not see the theme park as the greatest invention since the Roman arch.

It would be nice to say that the airhead aesthetic that postmodernism encouraged has passed, and much of it has. Its fate has been to become the style of choice for shopping centers and for slip-covering skyscrapers, and particularly for remodeling the first generation of malls, which now sport a new set of fashion clichés. As the expression of a residential vernacular, however, this kind of postmodernism seems here to stay; it is the perfect vehicle for a wishfully invented way of life and the buildings that serve it. Composed of equal parts of nostalgia, superficiality, and calculated guile, the style works best for those unfamiliar with the sources being ineptly or ludicrously caricatured. There is no denying the fact that it has become a large part of the American landscape and the American dream. But to treat it as the leading edge of anything, however—much less, of architecture—is a misguided reversal of reason of an almost noble order. The worst excesses—and they are everywhere—rank with any of the more dismal failures produced by the tortured and exhausted principles of the modern movement in its later years. One begins to believe that banal is better.

When the successes of the theme park and the expediencies of the pop landscape are raised to cult status, when their example is offered by tastemakers as a model for buildings whose role and image are intrinsic to a different and more traditional set of needs and values, or are used to bypass tough solutions to nontraditional problems, something very peculiar occurs. You get faux populism as high art. I think the word "faux," or "fake," fits; it is everywhere today, because it is so right for what is so wrong. Skewed in meaning, rather than indicating falseness, it gives a stamp of approval to the blatantly unreal, a suggestion of class to the frankly inferior. Using the French *faux* makes the fake chic; it gives the phony cachet. It goes with the same state of mind that sees architecture as gift wrap and accepts tarted-up history. Something real has been perverted, and something important has been abdicated. The result is faux architecture.

This is the state of mind that has made possible the drearier aspects of postmodernism—*pompier* works with Tootsie Roll moldings and cartoon cartouches, cardboard cutouts and paper-thin pretensions. These buildings are not witty and learned references to anything; they are caricatures, stand-up jokes, ponderous one-liners. The ineptness of scale and detail that makes these pastiche borrowings so ridiculous cannot be blamed solely on today's lack of formal traditional training. In fact, it hardly matters. Classical America, a devout group of Vitruvian believers, and the Prince of Wales's Institute of Architecture in London are working hard to correct this deficiency.

Actually, the genre of romantic recall is understood too well; the appropriation is extremely clever and appealing. We love those retro cottages and freshly minted Classical villas to which everyone can instantly relate without being to the manor and the money born; no matter that their expensively and consciously understated and overdone detail turns correctness into a too perfect grossness. These are the right settings for the life and costumes featured in newspapers' burgeoning fashion sections. The astutely selected esoteric feature is the mark of those in the chips and in the know. We admire glib contextual solutions that are as unreal and irrelevant as their fake stonework trim and as permanently meaningful as the next building cycle. We tolerate sloppy, free-fall history and surface novelties where paraphrase is considered an act of creative design and, supposedly, of irony and art. We accept the casual rip-off of punk Palladian skyscrapers with breathlessly overscaled, drop-dead lobbies above which everything else is shamelessly standard bottom-line. Games are being played, with marginally convincing results that are far less witty and wonderful than advertised. This theatrical pseudoarchitecture gets all the lines — praised, publicized, and generally accepted as the real thing.

Good—and great—buildings are being created today, but not in this way. Today's best buildings are as different from everything that has gone before as contemporary society, technology, life, and thought can make them. They carry compound images and messages. There are deeply embedded references to the past, but there is no flash-card history. Fiercely intellectual and subjective, they can be understood in many ways, on a wide range of user receptivity and response. Liberated from all doctrine and most restraints, they push the frontiers of art and experience; the freedom to soar or crash are equal possibilities. Because they figure so little in the public's consciousness or esteem, these remarkable buildings are being forced to occupy an unreal world of their own.

The inescapable reality is that the art of architecture today fits neither the American dream nor the American scene; this is a country in near-total architectural retreat. Many factors have fed this retreat, encouraging an architecture of facile illusion, of image over substance, of artifice over art. The death of Utopian modernism, in which social purpose, form, and function were revered as the holy trinity of style, has opened exotic paths for denial and escape. What disappeared as doctrinaire modernism lost credibility was not only faith in a certain way of building but also the purposes that kind of building was to serve: naive, idealistic, and even wrongheaded, architects still held that humanity and the environment were perfectable through design and that social contracts could be set and met. The modernism that was to be the instrument of salvation has long since been sidetracked or sold out, the dreams revealed as foolhardy; and the liberal philosophy and belief systems that supported the movement have been turned inside out, converted to the corrosive, politically correct agenda that entertains no discourse and takes no prisoners. The loss is less in the demise of a specific theory and system of building than in the collapse of the shared values and concerns that went with it.

With this loss has come a vacuum of the kinds of meaning and conviction that sustain connections to a larger place or purpose, that hold a society together. The society that modernism served was less fragmented and conflicted; the relatively homogeneous group that endorsed it is now viewed as a privileged, paternalistic minority establishing taste and standards for their own kind. That hierarchy has been blown to bits by today's polarized diversity of social and cultural standards, education, behavior, and opportunity. This is not a society that architecture can serve or represent in any monolithic way. There are architect activists in storefront offices battling inequity and decay, while others have withdrawn completely to the ivory towers of the more esoteric realms of philosophy and art.

In response or reaction, there has been a conspicuous turn inward, away from society, to an examination of self, often so intimate and narcissistic as to be incomprehensible without a set of clues. Visionary introspection has always had its place; architecture would be infinitely poorer without it. The Italian architect Aldo Rossi has created an unforgettable, iconic landscape of towers, flags, cabanas, and skeletal steel structures that both delight and disturb in their juxtapositions of almost childish gaiety and lonely isolation. In this country, John Hejduk's Masques are imaginary settings that use the

Architect John Hejduk's "masques" consist of narrative illustrations and lyrical text that go beyond the built world of reality to create extraordinary, imaginary places of myth and mystery. Drawing from The Thirteen Watchtowers of Cannaregio.

Derived geometries and symbolic references are cultivated over a more pragmatic and mundane reality in Peter Eisenman's buildings. Meaning and function can be elusive; stairs and columns have a life and logic of their own at the Wexner Center for the Arts at Ohio State University. *Photo courtesy of the Wexner Center.*

most seminal and suggestive building forms to illustrate universal stories of mystery and solitude as troubling as our times, as haunting as our dreams. This unbuilt architecture transcends the reality of construction to make the reality of our lives more poignant; it uses architecture as a narrative vehicle of powerful poetic communication.

But the self-absorption of the present generation has contributed to a dismissal of social needs in favor of arcane aesthetic exercises and narrow investigations of an intensely self-indulgent and almost uncommunicable nature. One questions their value, beyond self-satisfaction. Only at this moment of retreat and introspection could a talent like Peter Eisenman's have flourished and had a following. He has created a theoretical, abstract architecture in which the building is its own meaning and reward, an autonomous and arbitrary geometry generated by rationalizations of equally abstract and arbitrary features of the site, or chaos theory, or whatever is the latest vogue. The logic behind the geometry can be derived from projections of the history and geology of the setting, a logic as insistently abstract and intellectualized as the design itself. And only in this climate could the official opening in 1989 of Eisenman's Wexner Center for the Arts at Ohio State University be held with no art displayed at all—the empty building was its own exhibit—in a deliberate flouting of purpose and willful affirmation of its completeness as a work of art. It is currently undergoing a kind of retrofitting of commissioned, site-specific works that may, or may not, herald a new relationship between the artist and the museum.

These buildings can be seductive, even dazzling; we admire them for their artfulness while conceding their incompleteness or contrariness as architecture, but rarely is this enough to offset the clash of traditional purpose and creative arrogance so defiantly embraced. The fact that a building is explained as a projection of the site's history, or of preexisting conditions, or of natural topography does not validate the result unless it also serves program and purpose as effectively as it proclaims its own elegantly esoteric identity. If it fails that test, it not only fails to deal with architecture's most demanding challenge but also alienates those for whom it is intended and at least partially negates its usefulness. These buildings impress with their virtuosity, but they are rarely user-friendly, no matter how clever or handsome their intricate compositions and site relationships. That they frequently and fashionably rely on a "text," preferably of elaborate incomprehensibility, is quite beside the point. Their social role is clearly not at the top of their agenda.

When an intellectual performance becomes a denial of, or replacement for, architecture's primary purpose, or makes that purpose singularly difficult to carry out, signals are being sent. This kind of design goes beyond the process of exploring new ways to conceive and build that break down established traditions and old habits for innovative aesthetic and functional solutions. We are being told that it has become more important for architecture to be than to serve, to send messages than to fill needs, to exist as an art object in itself than to be integrated through its art into the rich and complex totality of life and use that makes this the most far-reaching art of all. From there it is not far to the revolutionary claim that architecture can completely reject its intrinsic nature as a social art because of the antisocial nature of the times. If a humanistic, sociological definition was tied to modernist principles, these are timeless considerations that remain at the core of the building art. Architects relinquish that role at the peril of being marginalized.

The dictum that form follows function was also intrinsic to modernism, given equal billing with its social role. Today this idea is not only questioned, it is actively rejected. While far from defensible as an automatic and exclusive generator of solutions, and now considered an innocent approach to a complicated process, it is a principle that has held long and influential sway over all aspects of design. If this was a simplistic attitude that failed to acknowledge many factors and conditions, it still suggested a rational connection between art and use, a direct relationship of program, structure, and form; its logic prevented many abuses. Eugène Emmanuel Viollet-le-Duc, the enormously influential nineteenth-century French architect for whom reality meant the functional stone-on-stone construction of the medieval buildings he admired so much, set the mood and the morality for the next hundred years. "A thing has style," he declared, "when it has the expression appropriate to its use." Style now stretches and even contradicts that definition; style has become divorced from both use and structure; style is its own excuse for being.

Today form follows feeling. Desire was the suppressed word for both the Victorians and the modernists; today desire, not utility,

Under the banner of postmodernism, Philip Johnson became the master builder of eclectic illusion. His fairy-tale skyscrapers in free-range styles include a stepped-gable tower for Houston's RepublicBank Center, *top,* and mirror-glass Gothic for PPG Industries in Pittsburgh, *bottom.* Johnson-Burgee, architects. *Photos,* Richard Payne

dictates design. Style responds to a different purpose and vision. Style is dream, invention, wish fulfillment. "Appropriate" is in the eye and mind of the creator and/or beholder, and the definition changes with the dream. We invent ourselves, our settings, our lives. Here, indeed, the real fake and the fake fake collide. An English actor, Eric Idle, on a visit to New York to make a film, marveled at the absolute confluence of real and false identity. Assuming that a policemen on the set was an actor, he asked what he'd been in recently. When the reply was "the homicide squad," Idle professed to be unsure whether that meant a TV series or a job description. Off the set is still on the set. "On the streets of New York . . . you cannot be sure . . . who is real and who isn't," he observed.[3] The look can be recycled unisex or Manhattan cowhand; grandmothers sport the gear of fluorescent, spandex-clad roller bladers; the outer limits of street style camouflage Ivy Leaguers; the improbable courtesan takes orders in the coffee shop. Identity is a product of the mood and the moment; the persona is the clothes that hang in the closet.

Is it any wonder, then, that we expect our architecture to do the same? To put on an identity, to create an image, a place, a world? Philip Johnson, in partnership with John Burgee from 1967 to 1991, rode this kind of facile eclecticism to enormous success, giving banks, manufacturers, and real estate developers skyscrapers with instant images and period trappings so interchangeable that the effect was always of a joke being played on whatever they pretended to emulate—mirror Gothic in Pittsburgh, Flemish stepped gables in Houston, false mansards for New York. History used like wallpaper trashes both history and architecture. It is fashionable to say that a hallmark of our culture is that it self-destructs; everything is expendible, renewable with the latest model. But buildings? In spite of their size, these structures hardly command a second glance. There is something so flat, so lacking in density and conviction, that their offensiveness virtually evaporates; they fail even at being seriously awful. Cities of strength, like Chicago and Boston, mock themselves with a foolish fashion parade on the skyline. Occasionally, however, there is an absolutely fortuitous union of client and container; Johnson and Burgee's little stretch skyscraper for the Museum of Television and Radio in New York says it all about the pretensions to permanence of the most transient and weightless of the entertainment arts.

3 *New York Times,* Nov, 1990, iv:11.

Of all the arts, architecture alone is not a studio, or an audience, art; it is a balance of structural science and aesthetic expression for satisfactions that go far beyond the utilitarian, and that only art can supply. The ways in which the equilibrium between the physical and the spiritual is resolved through building, the essential mix of efficiency and delight, the quality of the balance achieved and the degree to which this solution elevates the viewer's sense of self and place, are of primary and timeless importance. Great architecture speaks to body, mind, and soul, to the individual and to society as a whole. To substitute sentiment, esoterica, or elitist conundrums for this kind of total creative engagement trivializes architecture; it is a denial of the essence of building. To say that architects cannot meet current challenges because they are so overwhelming, or offer answers because the problems are insoluble, or that architecture is simply an instrument of investors who set the rules, is a cop-out; it makes architecture a dead art. To design without the challenge and discipline of solving real problems is to go beyond triviality to irrelevance. To speak of background buildings versus signature buildings turns context into a visual game, instead of an accomodation with history and society; it reduces the city to absurdity.

Eduard Sekler, professor emeritus of architecture at Harvard, reminds us that each generation, in its search for solutions, reformulates the problems; that is where and how new architecture begins. Without the old rules, the basic elements of building are being reconstructed in many different ways. Architecture is literally being taken apart and put back together again. Purpose, place and plan, structure, space and surface, solid and void, transparency and solidity, expression and suppression, perception and meaning—all are being subjected to intensive scrutiny and analysis, to renewed investigation and interpretation.

This architecture pursues common objectives but follows no party line. It is not going to "pull together" into a homogeneous post-postmodernist style or whole; nothing so neat or conventional is about to happen. A chaotic and pluralistic culture, the architect's rich array of personal choices, make this assumption a dated and deluding idea. Even sacred cows die. Art history's traditional methods of iconographical identification and analysis crippled, and then killed, the International Style by making the Procrustean bed that cut off all but its most formal, surface characteristics. This practice continues, not surprisingly, as critics and academics vie to find the next certifiable trend; "movements" keep spilling into the press and onto the symposium circuit.

The new work has enormous diversity and vitality. Its range includes the brilliant eccentricities of the late James Stirling in Great Britain, who, until his untimely death in 1992, pioneered an accomodation between history and modernism in a series of buildings of quirky originality and demonstrable greatness that have been an unending source of surprise. It has room for the consistently masterful and recondite minimalism of the Portuguese Álvaro Siza, with its subtle, mannerist inventions. It embraces the Japanese Tadao Ando's explorations of the connections of light and space to spirit, as well as the work of the American Frank Gehry, who pushes the relationship between sculpture and architecture to innovative and rewarding limits. The languages chosen may range from deco revivalism to stringent high-tech, but these practitioners are not the strange bedfellows they may seem. What they have in common, along with a growing number of their peers, is that all are engaged in the basic reformulation of how enclosure, light, color, form, space, and movement can be manipulated to solve problems of use and symbolism in unprecedented ways. Each reassembles the building from a very personal point of view.

This free but rigorous exploration is the single factor that unifies all of today's open-ended ideas and images. The search is never purely pragmatic; it is characterized by creative impulses and aspirations that move architecture on to a place where it has not been before. Today's architects are drawing on an enormous contributing range of historical, technological, and philosophical sources, inconceivable in any previous age. This is not academic borrowing in any conventional or historical sense, and it is not Disney "imagineering." A process of analysis and synthesis, light-years beyond cosmetic lifestyle simulation or popular market products, is revolutionizing architecture in our time.

The New Architecture

previous pages: James Stirling broke with modernism, reuniting the past and the present in a personal and innovative style. Staatsgalerie, Stuttgart, Germany. *Photo, Richard Bryant-Arcaid, courtesy of the James Stirling Foundation.*

Only the outrageous gets attention today, and the outrageous in architecture has a limited usefulness. Without the accelerated shock appeal that keeps other art forms in the public eye, the audience for innovative buildings, or for building as an art form, consists largely of professionals or patrons; it barely reverberates with the general public. The new architecture may be the best-kept secret in the arts.

It is safe to say that virtually no one coming out of architecture school now is working in what is conventionally known as the modernist or postmodernist style. What they are doing, however, is firmly rooted in modernism; there is no way to unlearn or renounce that revolution in structure and technology or its practical applications. To call it neomodernism suggests a revival or more of the same old thing with a few new twists. But this is a modernism carried farther and significantly transformed. Every premise about the art of building and the nature of the environment is being examined and overturned or restated in some drastically revised form. An era of unrestricted exploration has followed modernism's rigid limits and postmodernism's partying with the past. Means and objectives are being reformulated within an expanded philosophy and methodology of the building art. The transition has been made to a post-postmodernism of almost unlimited inventive variety.

What these architects are doing, in a sense, is reinventing architecture. They are stretching the limits of the art, much as Mannerism and the Baroque stretched the principles of the Renaissance, forever altering its vocabulary and range. Art never stands still; creativity is voracious—it either absorbs, appropriates, and transforms the past or swallows it whole to "advance" on some other front. Nor can art retreat, shedding "mistakes" to recapture some earlier innocence or perfection, as the enemies of modernism would have us believe. To ignore the present, to remain uninvolved with actuality, is to deny all that is vital and alive and intrinsic to a late twentieth-century art and style. The present always falsifies repetitions of the past, which become tainted or flawed to a greater or lesser degree; the past always fuels something new.

Released from bondage to both modernism and classicism—the pivotal traditions of the West—the new architecture operates in a world of expanded perceptions and ideas. Searching and provocative, it deals with the new through whatever means it finds to employ, devising ways to open or push and reshape the restricted envelope of modernism, breaking precedent, synthesizing these experiments for a product that reveals and celebrates a new approach to seeing and using space. Whatever the underlying philosophical consistencies, the solutions are personal and subjective, expressive of an individual taste and vision. The result is diversity—pluralism with a difference—but what unites it all is a shared purpose and method, similar questions asked and answers sought, reinterpretation beyond conventional eclecticism, a style beyond "styles" that speaks to a basic redefinition and restructuring of architecture for our time.

The best of this work is neither simple nor soothing, but neither is the world we live in. It offers no familiar fast fixes. It is not the postmodernist posturing or classical backpedaling taking place on the celebrity skyline. Its practitioners are not engaged in some giant ideological battle, with Prince Charles and his followers in a lifeboat desperately clutching the tried and true and rowing madly for some familiar shore, while others push off in a spaceship for the vast unknown. These architects explore, transcend, and even capitalize on some of the routes of retreat from modernism in pursuit of myth, nostalgia, and meaning; they are involved in probing investigations of a complex and challenging nature. Once the door had been opened to the breaking of modernist taboos—against history, against ornament, against symbolism and the enrichment of forbidden sources—architecture was able to rewrite programs and stretch the senses by acknowledging the achievements and influence of both the near and distant past in solutions that dare to cross the boundaries of all the arts. I would argue that this is the most dramatic, challenging, innovative, and important architecture to be produced in a long time, that it is a not-so-gentle revolution, but that it is also a revolution going unnoticed even in the intellectual circles where such things are charted, and is, in fact, being largely ignored. Unlike the modernist revolution, this radical work does not build its strengths by breaking with the past but, more like the Renaissance, transforms its sources through a brilliant synthesis, with far-reaching influence and effect.

As yet, fortunately, no name has been coined that sticks or that can cover an expressive range from weightless transparency to monumental solidity, from romantic imagery to high-tech rigor; labeling and codification, so dear to academics and tastemakers, lock in false limits and destroy exceptions and nuance. The chroniclers of the International Style treated Alvar Aalto gingerly and selectively, and ultimately left him dangling ambiguously because he did not fit

Light spills down the central stair that ties galleries and offices together in Stirling's Sackler Museum at Harvard University in Cambridge, Massachusetts, *top,* in a plan that opens the cramped site and transforms the small scale. *Photo, Richard Bryant-Arcaid; Entrance elevation rendering, bottom, and axonometric drawing, across page, courtesy of the Sackler Museum.*

into the established taxonomy. He was, of course, a far greater architect than many of those who did. As at any moment, good and bad coexist and are fed by the same stream. Like all styles, this one carries with it the baggage of the beliefs and norms of the society that informs and consumes it. What is peculiar to this moment is that the politically and aesthetically correct position that rejects quality as an elitist concept and denies judgment as "the privileging of the eye" has come together with an equally fashionable taste for the trashy and trendy to give us junk architecture. Like junk bonds, it has been overwhelmingly popular. It sells well and gets all the media lines. It is so seductively simple, even though schlock value, like celebrity, is a fifteen-minute thing. And it has successfully distracted attention from architecture that is less "accessible" and makes more demands on the "eye" that is currently being so perversely and ludicrously denied. It can be unsettling, although anything that is not unsettling about art and society today truly escapes reality.

What is offered here is a sampling of this new work, which is already well established; its practitioners span two generations and several continents. The representation and the emphasis are frankly uneven, because I write about buildings I have visited and seen. I maintain that anything else is critical fiction: photographs lie or, at best, misrepresent; it is so easy to invent a stylistic story line. It is my strong belief that one cannot understand a building without direct contact, experience, and response; there is simply no substitute for being there. My gaps and omissions imply no bias; more limited appraisal reflects my more restricted encounters with some admirable work of which I hope to see more. If the selection appears odd or arbitrary, it is due to the limitation of this self-imposed rule. And while I am aware that there are other architects who deserve equally to be included, everyone discussed here is a prime generator of the new. The examples chosen, while incomplete, suggest the range and character of what is happening on a more universal scale.

No architect has been a more significant agent of change than James Stirling, of the London firm of Stirling and Wilford, whose career was cut tragically short by his untimely death in 1992. Hindsight makes his work of the 1960s (in collaboration with James Gowan) and 1970s look less like the postmodernist vanguard, as it was hailed at the time, than a far deeper and more radical reordering of the building art. Like so many who followed

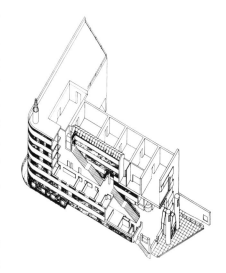

modernism, Stirling felt free to experiment with different "styles," to explore their imagery in very personal and contemporary terms. Whether it was the high-tech Engineering Building for Leicester University (1959–1963) or the Cambridge University History Faculty Building (1964–1967) those daring, conspicuously failed structures where concept, budget, and technology were so far apart that the buildings broke down completely—or the historical revisionism and superb urban planning of the internationally acclaimed Stuttgart Staatsgalerie (1977–1983), we now see a remarkable breakthrough of underlying consistency.

Stirling was a prodigious talent. No one since has equaled the synthesis of tradition and modernism that he pioneered at that significant moment when modernism lost its authority and history could be studied again. His style was so personal as to be inimitable, but his influence has been pervasive. Perhaps no one has changed architecture quite so much since Robert Venturi's postmodern manifesto of 1966, *Complexity and Contradiction in Architecture,* called for the breaking of rules and the rediscovery of enrichment. Stirling's work was no dilettante pastiche, however, no doctrinaire borrowing; he reclaimed traditional materials and reshaped historical details for his own purposes—and they were unlike anyone else's, at any time. From the robust mannerism of Michelangelo to the romantic classicism of Boullée, he had an intriguingly eclectic taste and idiosyncratic take on every source he admired. Never literal, his historical references demonstrated not the truisms of traditional details and construction, but their dramatic and magical possibilities in other contexts, for other suggestive and symbolic purposes.

At the time of his death, the critic Suzanne Stephens paid tribute to "the power of his transformative genius with the full range of architectural vocabulary, whether it belonged to a modern, industrial vernacular or traditional, classical language…his [more experimental] designs always contained those seeds of greatness that linked us to architecture's past and to its future."[1] He was uniquely at home with what the poet John Hollander has called "the immensely complex dialectic of the past and present [that] is of the ultimate essence for poetic originality."[2]

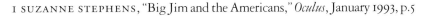

1 SUZANNE STEPHENS, "Big Jim and the Americans," *Oculus,* January 1993, p.5

2 JOHN HOLLANDER, "The Poetry of Architecture," *Bulletin of the American Academy of Arts and Sciences,* Februrary 1996, p. 32.

The dramatic, drum-shaped outdoor court of Stirling's Staatsgalerie in Stuttgart is part of a skillful design that carries the complex across changes in topography to unify the site. *Photo, Richard Bryant-Arcaid, plan and sections courtesy of the James Stirling Foundation.*

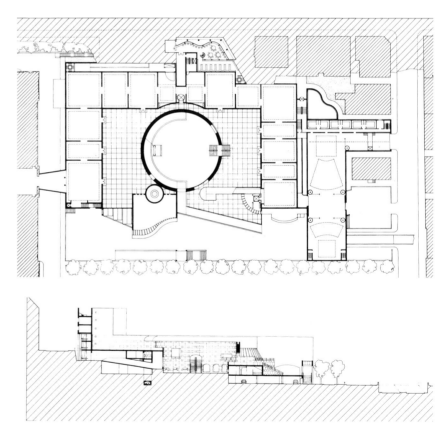

When this breadth of reference and original vision is passed through an intensely modernist sensibility, it leads to something totally new. Stirling pushed modernism to mannerism and turned some modernism upside down. His columns may not support—original sin in modernist doctrine; they can be freestanding and backlit for the sole purpose of suggesting an illusory scale that will create the feeling of monumentality where space precludes it, as on the woefully cramped site of Harvard's Sackler Museum (1979–1984). This is a kind of magic that only architecture can deliver. A stair is not treated as a formal route to a single destination with a routinely understood purpose; Stirling has used it both as a unifier of physical functions and as a visual device that gathers them into an illuminated stage set where the action takes place. (The great precursor for this dramatic role is Charles Garnier's monumental stair for the Paris Opera [1862–1875].)

Stirling was an ardent and unconventional colorist whose clients worked hard to tone down his strong signature green and his passion for colored exterior banding as rich as any Victorian monument's. These facade treatments were usually reduced to dull modulations of brick where exuberant striping was intended. Used well, as in the two-tone banding of the great drum stair of the exterior courtyard in Stuttgart, with its encircling parade of classical statuary, the result equals the best urban achievements of the past. "Stirling green" erupts everywhere in his work and can be annoyingly distracting in a gallery setting. But his vibrant colors can also be joyful and welcoming; the rainbow portal that invites one at the top of the stairs of the Clore Gallery for the Turner Collection (1980–1985) at London's Tate Gallery suggests that we might be entering Oz. That we are actually delivered into an environment of cold oatmeal when the Gallery opened, was due to the Tate's preference for porridge to the Stirling palette. The great Turners seemed to disappear into the mush, proving that too much caution can be as dangerous as too much exuberance.

The strength of Stirling's best work derives from his conceptual visualization of a building not as a sequence of conventionally linked separate rooms or spaces, but as a totality, an immediate whole, understood instantly and completely in all of its parts and relationships. This gives his work enormous resonance. Even with revisions and the subsequent refinement of details, the concept always held. This unique sense of multidimensional form and space characterizes his work in all of its stylistic guises; it was

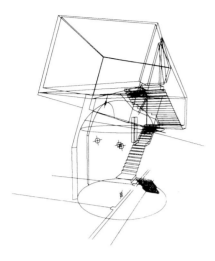

From a generation of innovators in California: Eric Owen Moss's computer-assisted design for "The Box," an angular, abstract, rooftop conference room in Culver City.

evident even in such earlier commissions as the School of Architecture Extension at Rice University in Texas (1979–1981), where it enlarged the limitations imposed by a restricted budget. Whatever his sources and however he used them, Stirling's exceptional vision was of a unified object in space and time. This brilliant conceptual synthesis, with its powerful spatial relationships, is the hallmark of truly great architecture—the single, consistent, enduring, and timeless feature that separates the masters from the dilettantes and decorators.

Like so much of the arts, architecture is an intense, closed, self-referential profession that operates internationally through a network of mutually shared interests and beliefs and edgy admiration. Bulletins of the new speed like an electric charge; the latest landmarks have visiting architects the way old buildings have mice. Communication is instant and incestuous, but with few exceptions the information and enthusiasm rarely go beyond the architectural cognoscenti and a specialized audience. In this country, a group on the West Coast has gathered around Frank Gehry, who has quite literally changed the shape of architecture as we know it. There is a common attitude and approach with a definite California tilt, but in no way is there a shared or uniform style. Thom Mayne and Michael Rotondi (formerly associated as Morphosis), Frank Israel, Eric Owen Moss, Stanley Saitowitz, Mark Mack, Peter Pfau, Wes Jones, Julie Eizenberg, Hendrik Koning, and Robert Mangurian are some of those on the Los Angeles–San Francisco axis that is the country's leading architectural edge. Whatever the common ideals, the work is extremely personal and even idiosyncratic; each architect has an individual, recognizable manner.

The expressionist, almost surreal manipulation of invented and metaphorical spaces of Eric Moss, the transforming, seductive recall of 1950s forms and colors by Frank Israel, the pursuit of an innovative and appealing high tech by Craig Hodgetts and Ming Fung— each in its own way transcends the usual or expected, challenging the mind and the eye. Thom Mayne celebrates both technology and a nostalgic *modernisme*—an intriguing, impossible combination at any other moment—for a complex aesthetic of angled, layered, and rotated planes and spaces. The intention is no less than to provide a new set of coordinates—a new starting place for design—by separating and studying all of the building's visible parts and uses, giving equal importance to formal components and service tech-

An ingenious and artful use of standardized elements by Hodgetts and Fung distinguishes the "Towell" Library, *top,* the temporary replacement for the Powell Library of the University of California at Los Angeles during construction changes. The Goldberg/Bean house by Frank Israel, *middle,* 1950s modernism is the nostalgic generator of a new style. *Photo, Grant Mudford.* Thom Mayne's intricate steel and concrete buildings are conceived as part of the natural terrain. The Diamond Ranch High School in Diamond Bar, California, *bottom,* contours a hillside for the school and its playing fields; a circulation spine divides the structure and connects the teaching spaces. Morphosis, with Thomas Blurock, Architects, associated.

nology, with each element receiving conscious design emphasis. In construction, this produces an architecture of great conceptual and decorative intensity; plan, structure, and detail merge in a rich, dynamic intricacy. The drawings, independent works of art in themselves, are evocative abstractions, crisp and elaborate, sometimes as baffling as they are beautiful. On the East Coast, the New York architect Steven Holl practices a more restrained revisionism, but he is equally concerned with the way buildings are understood and designed as a multisensory experience. He speaks of "the duration and perception of time, water, sound, the world of touch, proportion and scale,"[3] of a kind of building in which temporal and spatial responses are fused. In Helsinki's Finnish Museum of Contemporary Art (1996–1998) he has used the effect of the changing seasons as elements of the design.

Some of this architecture claims, or is saddled with, references to fashionable linguistic and literary theory, most conspicuously to phenomenology and deconstruction ("decon" to architecture groupies.)[4] It is a dubious debt at best, but the better work survives the burden put upon it. Whatever the philosophical arguments— and they are numerous and endless—the way building is analyzed and designed today is a direct response to the almost unprecedented stylistic freedom of a liberated, discontinuous, and pluralistic culture, where established rules and canons are being challenged or simply not known or acknowledged. The search for ways to understand and accommodate this culture has only the most tenuous and artificial connection to current academic French thought or other theories in vogue.

Fragmentation in life and art is the norm; breaking down and differentiating among the building's parts has become common practice. What characterizes decon is the recombination of these elements in a particular way: sharply angled plans that feature diagonal divisions and slanted walls dependent for their effect on a denial of gravity

New York architect Steven Holl arranges solids and voids in a style of reductive simplicity for the Mahuhari Housing in Chiba, Japan. *Photo, Paul Warchol.*

3 "Questions of Perception: Phenomenology of Architecture," *A + U* special issue, July 1994.

4 The exhibition "Deconstructivist Architecture," held at the Museum of Modern Art in New York in 1988, had the dubious distinction of naming and killing a style almost simultaneously. Sponsored by Philip Johnson, apostle of the new for the Museum since his International Style show in 1932, it united a group of talented architects by the most superficial visual aspects of their work. It was a failed cultural coup that included Frank Gehry, Zaha Hadid, Wolf Prix, Rem Koolhaas, Peter Eisenman, and Bernard Tschumi.

and perpendicularity. The look is jazzy and irresistibly on the cutting edge. To ignore stability in architecture requires a certain insouciance, since the history of the building art is based on the idea of keeping structures upright despite the unrelenting forces of gravity and the immutable nature of the materials involved. To follow this willful course, it is necessary to disguise and distort the rules of construction for an eye-catching frisson. It is an evasion that requires complex and indirect methods of support, preferably an elaborate cat's cradle of guy wires shooting off in all directions. A little of this can go a long way.

One of the originators of this manner is a talented Austrian, Wolf Prix, of the Vienna-based firm Coop Himmelblau, who has opened an office in Los Angeles; the free California climate is more congenial than tradition-bound Old World culture. Perhaps its most gifted and controversial practitioner is the Iraqi architect Zaha Hadid, who works in London, producing dazzling designs and exquisite drawings for buildings that are like hard, faceted jewels. Her acutely angled plans explore a kind of dynamic space beyond the possibilities of a conventional orthogonal approach. A 1983 competition-winning design for a luxurious residential club on Hong Kong's Victoria Peak electrified the profession with drawings of remarkable beauty and vitality that promised something intriguingly new. Her first constructed building, a fire station commissioned by the Vitra furniture company for its distinguished architectural enclave at Weil-am-Rhein in Germany, has set a record both for the number of its visitors and the number of working drawings the building required; every extraordinary angle had to be thoroughly detailed. Sleekly beautiful and ceaselessly provocative, the fire station has received international attention since its completion in 1993. The firefighters eventually moved out, and the building was scheduled to become a museum.

Hadid's many competition-winning designs have become well published and much admired icons rather than completed construction. The Cardiff Bay Opera House in Wales, a winner twice over, was killed by the British government's failure to assign any share of the lottery money awarded to cultural projects. Funds went instead to such safe and earnest endeavors as Kew Gardens's plan to preserve every available living species of plant life on the planet. The British establishment, strong on the worthy and stodgy, has a hard time endorsing creativity, and where it tries, it usually puts its wrong-headed bets in the wrong places. The

The provocative design of a fire station for the Vitra Furniture Company in Weil-am-Rhein, Germany, by the London-based Iraqi architect Zaha Hadid, pushes the limits of theory and design into a dynamic asymmetry beyond conventional structure and space. Interior view, exterior detail, perspective drawing. *Photos, A.L. Huxtable.*

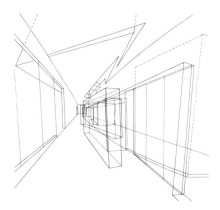

French, in contrast, tend to pursue the thrill of the new with confidence even in the highest places.

Hadid's buildings seem winged; they fly into space. In contrast, Frank Gehry's are carefully earthbound, studied and restudied through models and computer drawings[5] until their precise, striking forms take on the aspect of sculpture wedded to the site. Separating and reassembling the building's components more literally than many others, he carefully reshapes each function. Gehry has chosen a particularly difficult path—walking the thin, treacherous line where architecture crosses sculpture, where forms responsive to function take on shapes of autonomous beauty—as he pursues the tantalizing prospect of a union between the two arts. This precarious process involves a fair amount of public suffering, displayed engagingly to those who follow his work, as well as painstaking private investigation. The constant balancing act between on-the-edge experiments that renew architecture, and the potential disaster of architecture for sculpture's sake, can enlarge the art of building magically or diminish it disastrously, enrich it or empty it out. Gehry is literally pushing architectural limits in a dangerous but exhilarating game.

However eccentric or arbitrary these shapes may appear, they are the result of an obsessive and meticulous investigation of ways to house and express the building's functions through a marriage of the arts

---

5 The role of computer drawing in today's architecture cannot be underestimated; it actually determines much design. It not only facilitates immediate visualization of the work in three dimensions and from every possible angle, permitting a detailed study of design options never possible before, but it also eliminates the endless tracing and overdrawing by hand previously necessary. CAD and other computerized drawing and engineering programs have revolutionized both practical and visionary design possibilities and the production of working drawings. Printouts provide precise perspectives that clients can understand, as well as total and partially detailed views of minute accuracy and complexity. Beyond these routine advantages, the computer makes it easy to visualize, instantly and three-dimensionally, unusual shapes requiring complex engineering calculations that would be extremely difficult and impractical to translate into drawings and study models. The exploration of form as it is being done today was prohibitively costly and time-consuming and, in some cases, virtually impossible. Gehry utilizes a program originally developed in France for the aerospace industry and the design of the Mirage fighter plane; and while he says he does not like the computerized drawings that result, he uses it as a prime tool for the determination of his complex forms as well as for calculations for structural, material, and cost specifications.

A spare and elegant glass-and-steel addition, Sir Norman Foster's Sackler Galleries of the Royal Academy of Arts, London, *top,* dramatizes and enhances the historic brick-and-stone building. *Photos, Dennis Gilbert, courtesy of Sir Norman Foster and Partners.*

Richard Rogers's Channel 4 headquarters in London, *bottom,* derives an intricate imagery from sophisticated technology. The corner site affords a curved plan and open views. *Photos, A.L. Huxtable, plan courtesy of Richard Rogers Partnership.*

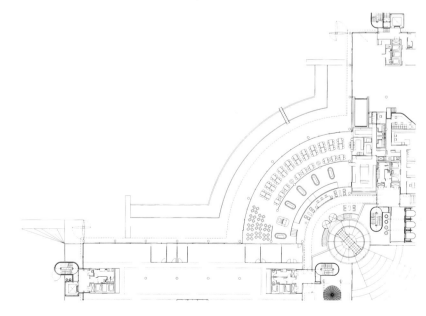

that Gehry so obviously loves. Working with Claes Oldenburg and Coosje van Bruggen, he incorporated Oldenburg's giant pop-art binoculars as the entrance to his building for the Chiat/Day Agency in Venice, California; he is friend, patron, and collaborator for many painters and sculptors. To be inside a Gehry house is to experience light, space, and color in a uniquely enriched and expanded way. His best buildings offer perceptions and pleasures hard to imagine before; they provide new dimensions to architecture and living. To these unconventional forms and spaces he adds a dedicated search for new materials and a fresh eye for older, more conventional ones that supply unconventional tone and texture. Much has been made of his early apotheosis of common chain link and plywood; today he is more likely to indulge in the costly elegance of copper sheathing. But this attention to surface is intrinsic to his innovative aesthetic. No facile art, this; it requires uncertain moves into unprecedented territory, accompanied by relentless self-criticism. One misstep and all is lost. Gehry loves the challenge, and even the danger.

The American Frank Gehry's work crosses the thin line between sculpture and architecture. The architect commissioned Claes Oldenburg and Coosje van Bruggen to adapt the sculptor's giant binoculars as the entrance for the Chiat/Day Agency in Venice, California. Frank O. Gehry and Associates, Santa Monica, California. *Photo, Grant Mudford.*

The British have been generous with commissions to well-established, highly respected practitioners of an earlier generation, Sir Norman Foster and Sir Richard Rogers. Both are modernists who work in a precise and rational high-tech manner, although their interpretations are poles apart. High tech, where flights of fancy are subject to the logic and proprieties of an engineering rationale, seems to suit the traditionally disciplined nature of the British character, if one dare make such an obviously superficial generalization. It dominates much of the new British work, whereas the French, to proceed on this slippery ground, seem to care less about the vocabulary chosen than about the stylishness of the look and the polemical rhetoric.

Foster's beautiful, finely honed, and perfectly polished details are evident in large and small works that include the radically reengineered concept of London's Stansted Airport (1981–1991) and the Sackler Galleries (1985–1991), the delightfully intimate addition to the Royal Academy of Arts in London that is a consummate demonstration of how an older building can be enhanced and dramatized by a modern intervention. Art and history are beautifully served by the new construction set into a court of the old brick building; the refinement of the connecting glass stairway and the glass elevator to the new top-floor galleries, marvelously sleek and subtle in their calculated transparency, make us delighted voyeurs of tradition as we take off into the future.

Rogers is best known for his controversial, kit-of-parts Lloyd's Building in London (1981–1986). In spite of his seriousness about technology, and his growing environmental preoccupation with "green" architecture, he treats his technological components in a playful and poetic way that has no counterpart. The transparent escalators at Lloyd's invite your observation of their mechanical parts, in color and motion, like toys for the eye. His buildings are immensely assured and superbly assembled. The Channel 4 Television Headquarters (1990–1994) delivers as much under-stated sophisticated theatricality as simple functionalism; the drama, however, is based on expert planning and an increasingly masterful use of technology. Stacked metal-mesh balconies just inside the faceted, reflective, plate-glass facade form exterior public corridors that everyone uses. This glass front, with its tense web of elaborate airy cables, is folded in a way that both opens and embraces the corner site. A gently curved plan eliminates the boredom of long, straight-lined halls and offices. There are views of the street and of a garden at the rear from most of the building. Deceptively simple details, such as a stair whose treads and risers, with lights along the wall, draw elegant lines and angles against a stark white backdrop, are unexpected and assured works of art. Whatever the off-the-rack look, however, all of this high-tech design relies on superb custom execution.

Much of the new British work continues in this vein, imaginatively and even exquisitely engineered. Younger architects like Nicholas Grimshaw and Partners update the idiom while layering it with a bit of selective nostalgia of their own. Grimshaw's spectacularly handsome addition and remodeling for the Channel tunnel railway terminal (1990–1993) at London's Waterloo Station is an impressive union of aesthetics and technology. These architects have bypassed pop art in favor of the classic modernism of Mies, Saarinen, and Eames, brought back from the dustbins of recent history to which they were consigned by now-aging Young Turks. Furnishings that are not custom-made are the once familiar but long-ignored Charles Eames and George Nelson designs of the 1960s—rediscovered, revived, and respected—and clearly loved. Work like this is in marked contrast to Britain's well-publicized, born-again classicists operating under royal sponsorship. But there are also free spirits like Will Alsop, who starts with a dedicated modernist base but breaks it wide open, infusing it with a highly personal energy and originality. His provocative designs combine the British love of high tech with an unconventional and visionary imagination and a strong painterly sensibility; his work, in which ingenuity and color play major roles, often starts with a painting. Alsop, like Stirling, is one of those charismatic, prodigiously talented, larger-than-life figures that the British have always produced and do their best to ignore.

In Portugal, Álvaro Siza operates on still another frontier. Rooted in modernism, he transcends modernism; his style has been described by the Italian architect and critic Vittorio Gregotti as a new minimalism;[6] one could call it a radical minimalism in its departures from received doctrine. His innovations are indeed radical; they have coincided with the liberating forces of postmodernism (and a postmodernist style that he heartily dislikes). But this does not begin to explain the complex interrelationships that are smoothly integrated into a deceptively simple whole. Siza begins where the modernists left off. There is homage to Le Corbusier—he, too, has been touched by the magical union of light and space of the church at Ronchamp. But he uses the clean, bare, reductive vocabulary established by the modern movement for a minimalism that expands, rather than restricts, architectural possibilities. His buildings are a fugue of orchestrated views and events. Although he draws from a Portuguese tradition of simple, traditional masonry, his eloquent walls speak a twentieth-century language. These strict geometries are the expressive tool for a much more fluid, plastic, volumetric, and kinetic approach to the making of architecture. Space has not been handled so theatrically since Mannerism; facades have not been composed so surprisingly since the eccentric Baroque of Nicholas Hawksmoor.

Entrance stair of the Galician Center for Contemporary Art in Santiago de Compostela, Spain, by the Portuguese architect, Álvaro Siza, employs a stringent mimimalism that subtly reorders perceptions. *Photo, Juan Rodriguez.*

In Spain, Rafael Moneo combines a sophisticated eclecticism with a committed modernism. He has built one of the most beautiful museums of our time, the National Museum of Roman Art (1980–1984) in Mérida, a Spanish town where one stumbles over classical ruins and runs headlong into Roman temples. An old Roman road runs right through the building and is incorporated into it. Soaring brick arches house the antiquities in a series of spectacular light-drenched spaces connected by open, galleried balconies for related secondary collections. In situ relics under the building have not been disturbed; here the enclosing arches are low, cryptlike and dark. The aesthetic unity of container and contents has an extraordinary magic.

6 VITTORIO GREGOTTI, "Thoughts on the Works of Alvaro Siza," *The Pritzker Architectural Prize 1992.*

Moneo has designed a completely different kind of art museum in Massachusetts, the Davis Museum and Cultural Center at Wellesley College (1989–1993). Open galleries are stacked around an enclosed central stair with walls of polished pale wood that glow like gold; one almost floats up the shallow steps between floors. Spacious, luminous galleries are visible and accessible from each landing; daylight spills through all of them from skylights at the top of the building, the light increasing in intensity as one ascends. Treated as a single volume layered with exhibition spaces, the structure is beautifully articulated and arranged behind a red brick facade. Moneo's expansion of the Atocha Railway Station in Madrid (1984–1991) also marries the sensitive and the spectacular. The great train shed and station are restored, while a new tower, parking structure, and connections to public transportation are in a sympathetic but distinctive style that neither upstages nor downplays the landmark terminal.

Among the younger architects in Spain, Enric Miralles practices a dynamic, free-form expressionism with high-tech overtones that recalls the work of Thom Mayne and the southern California school. Intricate, multilevel designs are derived from cues that exploit unconventional characteristics of the site—a riverbed, a road, a line of trees, even the physical marks of the land's past use—for surprising interiors, vistas, and circulation routes. This site-sensitive work delights in complex, interacting planes and sections that invent new kinds of space and invite new responses.

France has moved on dramatically from its early postwar postmodernism, when the rational, farsighted planning of its new towns coincided with a brutal *retardataire* modernism in which a tutti-frutti, space-age futurism battled with some extremely peculiar evocations of the past. Multicolor, high-rise artichokes and mirror-glass versions of Versailles brought antimodernism and antihumanism to the brink. Even Jean Nouvel, one of France's leading architects, built flying-saucer housing as late as 1985–1988 in the Roman town of Nîmes, whose inhabitants still seem stunned. Without giving up architectural brinksmanship, French design now stresses two modes: a nostalgic modernism and a sleek high tech. Like so much that is French, both styles are equally romantic, and like so much else today, both styles skirt the edge. Jean Nouvel's glistening, steel-and-glass designs are filled with complex and subtle ideas about light that a purely functional or technological rationale could never justify. His building for the Fondation

The National Museum of Roman Art in Mérida, Spain, *top,* and the Davis Museum and Cultural Center, Wellesley, Massachusetts, *bottom,* both the work of the Spanish architect, José Rafael Moneo, are designed, respectively, for a national collection of Roman art and a college collection of painting and sculpture. Timeless arcaded brick for the antiquities, and stacked, skylit white-walled galleries for the mixed works of many periods, share an underlying modernist sensibility. *National Museum of Roman Art photo, Lluis Casals; Davis Museum photo, Steve Rosenthal.*

Cartier in Paris (1991–1994) is a superbly polished gem. All-glass even to a glass wall at the street line, with the thinnest and most elegant metal cables supporting the idea of weightless transparency, the building invites multiple readings of its crystalline layers and prismatic perfection.

In contrast to Nouvel's exquisitely idealized technology, Christian de Portzamparc practices an equally inventive and nostalgic modernism. Called a humanist, a loaded word, he delights in subjective and evocative images, while seeking new ways of combining form and function into a different kind of whole—an assemblage of parts that can look deceptively like a trendy collage of 1950s shapes, colors, and details. Whether pure surface or a more profound message beneath it, effect is supreme in French architecture. Wit and style, symbol and metaphor, inform French philosophy and practice. The work of Philippe Starck raises common objects to haute couture; this is the art of the dernier cri.

The Dutch architect Rem Koolhaas, one of the most closely watched polemicists and paper architects on the international scene for many years, became a major player in the 1980s, when his radical structures began to appear in Holland, France, and Germany. The French, as noted before, unlike most nations at the policy-making level, tend to take the quantum architectural leap. With the decentralization of power from Paris to the cities, the mayor of Lille in a bid for the future awarded the commission for the master plan of Euralille, a hub of transit, business, and culture for all of Europe, to Koolhaas and his firm, OMA (Office for Metropolitan Architecture). Congrexpo, a combined concert hall, convention center, and exhibition space built by the firm as part of the plan, is described by Koolhaas as "scandalously simple," consisting of two separate concrete structures. "An enormous plane of concrete, deformed into a scallop shape...accomodates the concert hall; a concrete plate, folded according to the different auditorium slopes to become a bridge, forms the conference center."[7] The two elements are covered by a single roof, in a container of cool, industrial severity.

Continuous, fluid space connects one part of Koolhaas's buildings to another, through ramps, stairs, and canted surfaces that cut through

The glass walls of the French architect Jean Nouvel's Fondation Cartier in Paris, top, a jewel-like building of cool precision, play with light and reflection and complex ideas of layered transparency. *Photo, Philippe Ruault.* The Grand Palais, Lille, France, *bottom,* is a radical reordering of space and movement in a deceptively understated industrial container by the Dutch architect, Rem Koolhaas and the Office for Metropolitan Architecture.

7 OFFICE FOR METROPOLITAN ARCHITECTURE, REM KOOLHAAS, and BRUCE MAU, *S,M,L,XL*, (New York: Monacelli Press, 1995), p.1204.

146

Serene forms and mixed cultural references mark Arata Isozaki's Museum of Contemporary Art in Los Angeles, *top.* "The Spiral," by Fumihiko Maki, *bottom*, uses a complex, abstract geometry for the facade of a Tokyo store that also contains an art gallery on a spiraling ramp inside. *Photo, Botond Bognar.*

and dematerialize floors and walls. The radical rearrangement of conventional space and expectations that characterizes this unconventional approach is explained by Koolhaas in his description of the firm's competition entry of 1993 for the Bibliothèques Jussieu in Paris. "Instead of a simple stacking of floors, sections of each level are manipulated to touch those above and below; all the planes are connected to a single trajectory, a warped interior boulevard that exposes and relates all programmatic elements."[8] The visitor moves along a sequence of changing levels and vistas.

In Japan, the masters of modernism, Kenzo Tange and Fumihiko Maki, were joined in the 1970s and 1980s by a generation of postmodernists dominated by Arata Isozaki, whose work coincided with the greatest period of postmodernist turbulence. Isozaki's eclectic themes and references range from the inspirational curves of Marilyn Monroe to a historically and culturally disorienting version of Michelangelo's Campidoglio; the results are brilliant and sometimes disquieting architecture. In this country, the Museum of Contemporary Art in Los Angeles (1983–1986) is an accomplished work that combines an affectionate and knowing recall of some of the ambience of modernism's founding institution, the Museum of Modern Art in New York, with a series of dramatic galleries and the architect's signature barrel-vaulted space as its crowning feature. The exterior is faced in a beautiful red Indian sandstone.

Starting from a radical point of no return, a more recent generation in Japan has felt no need to prove its break with the past through historical acrobatics. These younger architects risk less; they feel free to reinterpret modernism in many ways. Toyo Ito stands out for his free and imaginative use of what once was a formally restrictive technological vocabulary. Tadao Ando eschews all postmodernist tricks for an archetypal architecture of geometry and light, for a minimalist, boldly reductive, forceful poetic vision. Eastern and Western traditions can no longer be separated in his work; strong affinities to Le Corbusier and Louis Kahn are fused with the Japanese visual and aesthetic heritage. Essential to his vision is the Japanese sense of the symbiotic relationship of the landscape and setting with the architecture, something he manipulates with singular drama and control. His buildings have a powerful geometric simplicity that emphasizes and evokes the emotional

8 Ibid., 1318–1323.

and psychological aspects of form, light, and space. "Even as a parade of postmodern work, Kabukiesque and iconographic, swept over the eighties," writes Katukiya Matsuba, "Ando practiced his stoic aesthetic with silent intent."[9]

Ten Buildings

The following, more detailed discussion of buildings by Ando, Siza, Gehry, and Portzamparc shows how architects of dramatically different styles and sensibilities share the common concerns, processes, and goals of the new architecture. All are buildings of uncommon beauty and intelligence that enlarge the definition of architecture in remarkable new ways. And nothing could be farther from the current preoccupation with turning places into "theme park–inspired imitation festive space and the hypothetical reality of advanced electronic environments."[10]

Siza's and Ando's works share a deceptive simplicity. But in spite of a mutual reliance on a vocabulary of basic geometrical minimalism, their buildings are not only anything but simple, they are also totally unlike. Siza indulges a sophisticated, almost cinematic sensibility; Ando pursues complexity by bringing opposites together in geometric forms that create "tension and the power to arouse emotion." He speaks of "the simultaneous expression of antithetical elements, such as the introduction of profoundly complex, labyrinthine space within clear and simple compositions;" he repeatedly uses, in Henri Ciriani's observation, "the box, cubic grid, segment of circle, cylinder, [and] cross…enriched by stairs and terraces integrated into contours of the landscape."[11] To this he adds the effects of water—natural lakes and manmade pools. But how different Ando's expression of the postmodern Venturian manifesto of "complexity and contradiction" is from Venturi's recondite exhortation of history and precedent to support painstaking intellectual solutions. Ando's invocation of "confrontation and conflict …the abstract and the concrete" may begin in the architect's mind and eye, but it ends as a strong visceral sensation for the viewer, a gut response intrinsic to the experience of all great buildings.

9 Guidebook accompanying the catalog for Tadao Ando exhibition at the Centre Georges Pompidou, Paris, 3 March–24 May 1993.

10 Ibid.

11 Ibid.

Ando likes to refer to himself as a loner, an outsider, a self-educated architect totally without formal training, with working-class roots in Osaka, where he is still headquartered in a handsome studio building of his own design, to which international commissions flow. He continues to claim the role of "guerrila," maintaining "an attitude of resistance toward existing social conditions."[12] But he is no self-taught innocent, as Francesco Dal Co rightly points out.[13] In those solitary trips to Europe in the 1960s that were his real architectural education, experiences that no classroom exercises can approach, his pilgrimage points were not only the great buildings of Western civilization or the obvious monuments of Western modernism, but also the more ambiguous, sensuous, transitional works of the Viennese Secession by Otto Wagner and Josef Hoffmann and that most esoteric icon, then and now, the house of the philosopher Ludwig Wittgenstein. The later modernists, he noted, "had nothing of the layered continuity and discontinuity present in [Adolf] Loos' architecture or the mysterious relationship between light and shadow present in traditional Japanese architecture."[14]

Nowhere is this preoccupation with the effects of light and shadow better illustrated than in Ando's Church of the Light (1988–1989), built in a residential suburb of Osaka. This small, spartan, concrete box is pure sorcery: it consists of a tiny triple cube, the rectangle cut into at a fifteen-degree angle by a freestanding wall. Entering the church through this sharply pivoted space, one must turn 180 degrees to face the front of the chapel and the altar, where a cross of light has been created by two intersecting, open slits running the full length and width of the altar wall. This light is magical and compelling. To reach the altar, and the light of the cross, one walks down a sloping floor to the front; rough wooden benches are made of the concrete forms from the building's construction. Light, in Ando's words and practice, is used not only for "its physical presence, but also its transcendental implications."[15]

12 TADAO ANDO, *GA Document Extra 01*, A.D.A. Edita Tokyo, 1995, 21.

13 FRANCESCO DAL CO, *Tadao Ando, Complete Works* (London: Phaidon Press, 1995), 7.

14 TADAO ANDO, *GA Document Extra, 01*, A.D.A. Edita Tokyo, 1995, 12.

15 HENRI CIRIANI, interview with Ando, *Visitor's Guidebook* accompanying the catalog of the exhibition of Ando's work at the Centre Georges Pompidou, May 1993.

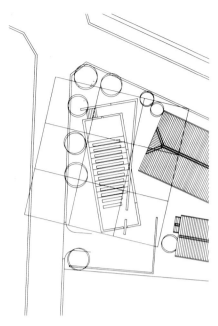

Tadao Ando's preoccupation with light, nature, and seasonal change adds a unique spirituality to his homage to western masters. The Church of the Light in Osaka, *right,* is a simple rectangle with the front wall slashed by a cross-shaped opening admitting the only light; an off-axis entrance *entrace, plan above,* makes one turn sharply to approach the cross, the light, and the altar. *Opposite page, far right, top and bottom,* a processional route along a path of closed, open, and screened spaces integrates a spectacular setting into the experience of the Children's Museum at Hyogo. *Photos,* Mitsuo Matsuoka. *Opposite page, left,* an open balcony and a closed, curving corridor encircle a high glass-walled space with an open court beyond at the Conference Center for the Vitra furniture company at Weil-am-Rhein in Germany. *Photos, A.L. Huxtable.*

The architect describes his Children's Museum in Himeji, Hyogo (1988–1989), as "forceful, geometric lines…inscribed in a natural landscape…a meditation on revitalizing the relationship between man and his environment, between man and architecture…man and nature."[16] His sketches impose these lines on the land with sweeping certitude. The visitor travels the length of a linked promenade of open walks, concrete walls, shallow pools, and breathtaking views of the surrounding hills above and lake below to the museum building, theater, and workshops. The voyage is interrupted halfway by an open, unroofed plaza with topless columns, in which the relationship between earth, sky, man, and building is intriguingly open-ended, as one contemplates the magnificent natural vistas. While the role of children in this complex seems uncertain to Western eyes (except for their liberation into a superb landscape and some programmed activities after close city quarters), the experience provided is universal. The soft green of the hills and the opalescent sheen of the lake were seen in mist and gentle rain by this visitor, with each new element of the architecture and landscape along the way mysteriously and magically revealed. On a sparkling day it would be another, and equally beautful, experience.

A less monumental building, the Conference Center for the Vitra furniture company (1992–1993), at Weil-am-Rhein, Germany, has a similar elegance at a much smaller scale. A narrow, gently curving corridor leads to a railed balcony overlooking a double-height space with a glazed wall through which one sees a walled courtyard outside. The sequence of shapes and the changes in scale are delightful, as are the contrast of beautifully formed and finished concrete walls and pale wood floors and the way light accentuates the spaces indoors and out; there is something of Alvar Aalto's sensibility in this use of natural light, materials, and colors, and skilled manipulation of scale. Small chairs scattered about appear to have been recently vacated; their random position provides a surprising touch of intimacy and a serendipitous aesthetic accent.

Álvaro Siza's Galician Center for Contemporary Art in Santiago de Compostela (1988–1993), in the far northwest corner of Spain, does much to define the state of architecture today. It definitely puts the

16 Ibid.

theme-park world of postmodernism behind us. Although it is inserted into the sacrosanct fabric of this famous pilgrimage town, there is no pretense to a false historical humility; the building's strongly angled forms and almost unbroken horizontal planes make a compelling case for the enduring validity of modernism. And yet the design is as respectful and contextual, if one may use that overworked and misused term, as it is modern, another word that has come to beg all meaning and definition, although it can still be understood in its historical sense as something distinctly of its own time. The building does not so much occupy the site as it is inserted into it; from a distance one does not see it at all. Yet the long, low structure has a dynamism that prefigures the surprises within the bold exterior forms.

Called a work of "preservation/transformation" by Siza's office, a dualism that collapses past and future together, the museum occupies a roughly triangular site surrounded by historic buildings that will be restored as part of the project. The site narrows to a twenty-one-degree angle at its tightest corner, dictating a striking, wedge-shaped plan with two L-shaped sections that converge and interpenetrate. The visitor enters up a short flight of steps, through an angled portico at the structure's small, sharp end. This entrance is neither as understated nor as inconspicuous as its size and location might suggest; there is an almost reverse high drama in the subtle precision with which the stair meets and stops a long porticoed ramp that sweeps along the main facade. Inside, the reception area is an oasis of cool white marble that features a striking serpentine counter. Where the two sections of the building merge, they form a full-height triangular atrium, flanked by exhibition galleries and an auditorium. A circulation core of stairs, ramps, and corridors slashes straight across the angled plan.

From this central space, shallow corner steps rotate down diagonally into a lower level of irregularly shaped, temporary-exhibition spaces; other stairs lead up to large, rectangular, permanent-exhibition galleries, with hovering soffits dramatized by light. But these are not the usual monumental stairs of the Beaux Arts tradition, paraphrased by Robert Venturi and Denise Scott Brown in their additions to London's National Gallery and the Seattle Art Museum. Siza's stairs are a vibrant run of pure form that controls a sequence of startling views that would have enchanted Dr. Caligari. The visitor becomes intensely aware of forms and dimensions of the most rigorous, artful invention, of a powerful and profound experience of architectural space.

The angled forms of the Galician Center for Contemporary Art at Santiago de Compostela in Spain by Álvaro Siza are reduced to dynamic minimalist simplicity; the long, low structure is held respectfully lower than the historical buildings around it. *Photo, Juan Rodriguez.* A tight, triangular site shapes the unusual plan.

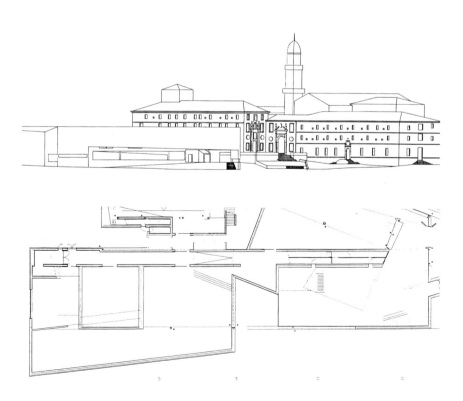

At the top of the stairs, one faces the pointed end of a corridor that divides diagonally for public galleries and private offices; this scissorlike split is knife-sharp in its diverging paths. Since the camera records such views as pure abstraction, the architect's office carefully labels photographs of them Top and Bottom. Siza's buildings are full of unusual revelations that seduce with their visual and poetic force. Unexpected, soaring heights, a dramatic wash of light from a suddenly discovered or elusive source, a sharply angled room or gently curving passage, a perfectly sculptured stair, become an embracing, aesthetic experience.

Sharply split corridors, *top*, and views across stairs, *bottom*, are pure abstractions created by by light, walls, and unexpected vistas. *Photos, Juan Rodriguez.*

In all of Siza's work, site and structures are part of a unified concept and landscape plan. The Faculty of Architecture of the University of Porto in Portugal (1986–1993) uses landscaping and continuous circulation ramps to tie two facing rows of buildings together. Four "matching" but unequal, rectangular pavilions that vary in height, shape, and fenestration march *enfilade* across the site, housing classrooms with spectacular river views; the subtle variations of their taut, abstract volumes play off against each other and the setting. Opposite, and joined by a fifth, offset building, a single long, low structure completes the complex and contains the school's other functions: auditorium, library, lecture rooms, and student facilities. The ramps run the full length of all the buildings, inside and out; they rise and fall and loop off to a semicircular exhibition area; there are views of the other buildings and the landscape along the way. In use, they set the whole into a kind of contrapuntal motion. Half a world and centuries away, the tradition of Thomas Jefferson's University of Virginia with its Lawn and Ranges has been radically updated.

The entrance to an earlier building for the Faculty of Architecture, the Carlos Ramos Pavilion (1985–1986), is a concise demonstration of Siza's spatial magic. Glass doors, placed asymmetrically at one corner of a U-shaped structure that has been bent into acute rather than ninety-degree angles, open onto a short flight of stairs widening almost imperceptibly from the point of the entrance to a double curve at the top, where corridors start on both sides. Siza marries mannerism and modernism in this one astounding little passage by the skilled manipulation of the surprising diagonal. This is a modernism containing bold departures and subtle complexities that highlight today's seismic shift in the philosophy and practice of architecture.

Detail of classroom building of
Siza's Architecture Faculty at the
University of Porto in Portugal, the
school features a row of individual
classroom pavilions and a single long
structure for student and academic
facilities united by a continuous
indoor and outdoor ramp.

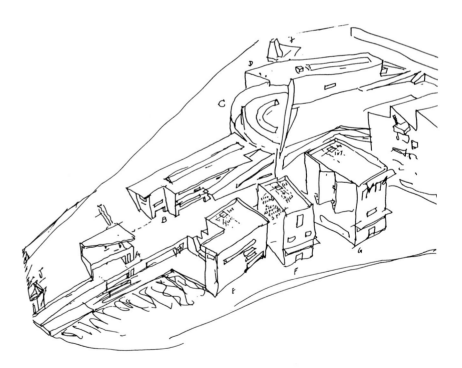

A series of remarkable structures charts Frank Gehry's radical, innovative course, beginning with his own house of 1978 in Santa Monica, where he literally surrounded and enlarged an older house with radical interventions of the infamous plywood and chain link. The shock and disapproval of his suburban neighbors has yielded to international acclaim and prestigious commissions. For one of his most ardent patrons, Rolf Fehlbaum of the Vitra furniture company in Germany, he has executed a number of buildings, including a museum of the manufacturer's products at Weil-am-Rhein that takes the visitor on an ascending spiral through luminous white spaces washed by natural light from above. The furniture, solitary or in groups, on pedestals and platforms or suspended in air, appears to be haloed, enthroned, and enshrined. Surely this is the apotheosis of the chair.

A headquarters building for Vitra (1988–1993), across the Swiss border in Basel, is one of Gehry's bolder and more colorful compositions. The plan combines conventional offices for a conservative sales operation with free-form administrative space, the two sections connected by a series of bridges crossing a full-height atrium at different floor levels. In a conventional building, one would simply get off an elevator on unrelated floors; here one is acutely aware of the passage from one part of the structure to another. The transition is not only a spectacular visual and spatial experience in its own right, but also emphasizes the drama of the transfer between areas that are totally unlike in use, look, and feel. The process of getting there has its own rewards.

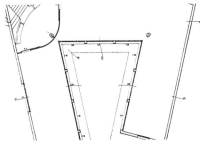

A corner entrance stair, angled and asymmetrical, widens from the bottom to a double curve at the top where corridors begin in Siza's artful manipulation of diagonals for illusory effect. *Photo, A.L. Huxtable.*

Chapel-like executive offices are placed within the conspicuously sculptured exterior. When I saw them, just before completion, the soaring spaces and painted walls glowed red or gold as natural light streamed from skylights and strategically placed windows. Altars would have seemed as suitable as desks and chairs. (How pervasive and lasting is the influence of Le Corbusier, how numerous are the echoes of his church at Ronchamp!) These rooms are exhilarating; at the same time, I responded uneasily to their subsuming of purpose to a superb but gloriously willful aesthetic. Gehry's evocative and sense-filling environment is a personal statement of tremendous conviction and power. And it works, in a wonderful, scary way.

For the American Center in Paris (1991–1994), Gehry was uncharacteristically conservative in his selection of exterior cladding, using the ubiquitous Parisian limestone as an act of contextual homage to the neighboring buildings. It is easy, in matters of French culture,

Opposite page, the sculptured exteriors of Frank Gehry's American Center in Paris, *top,* and the headquarters of the Vitra furniture company in Basel, *bottom,* are the result of painstaking functional analysis that underlies the striking shapes. The American Center's entrance is a Piranesian experience. *Photo, A.L. Huxtable.*

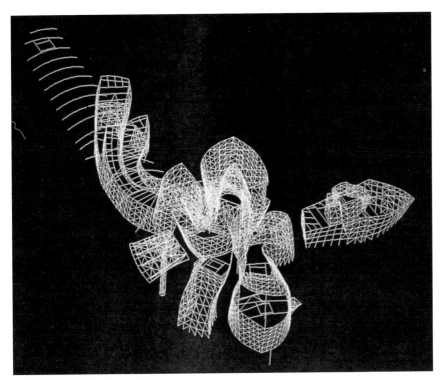

A branch of New York's Guggenheim Museum in Bilbao, Spain, *opposite page,* offers Gehry's boldest experiments in form and space. From the model, *top,* through construction, *bottom,* the unconventional design has been analyzed by computer for structural feasibility, engineering calculations, materials, and costs. Computer diagrams, *left,* show some of the detailed analysis of the design.

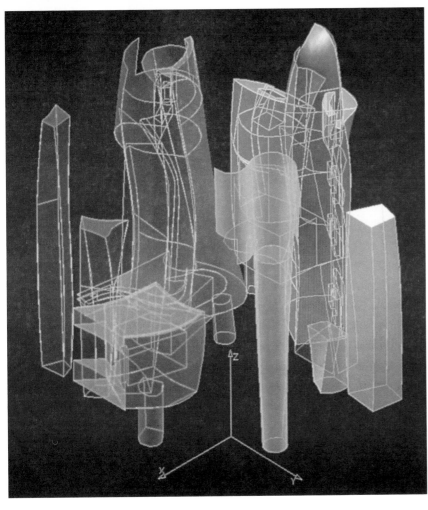

to confuse intimidation with respect. He admits that the gesture backfired. By the start of construction, most of the neighboring buildings had been torn down; by the end, the "context" was gone. The fallacy of contextualism, the masquerade of matched materials, the cosmetic cover-up of architectural *maquillage* meant to make a building "fit" surroundings that frequently change, are a trap into which many architects jump or fall through good intentions or self-delusion. However, the building's eccentric pileup of forms is barely tamed by the uniform stone skin; the interiors are marvelous adventures in space. But the muted result suggests, from the outside at least, that the real Gehry is struggling to get out.

Gehry buildings are becoming an instantly recognizable part of the international scene. They are all handsome, enriching, and surprisingly contextual, but, inevitably, questions arise. Such a compelling aesthetic can overwhelm the delicate and essential equilibrium between art and use that makes architecture a unique art. When is the responsibility for that balance abrogated? And does it matter when the architect is so gifted and the product so exceptional? How far can one go on this particular path without becoming too arbitrary or self-indulgent? When does the breakdown and reconfiguration of use become secondary to the invention of pure form? Functions can sometimes seem tenuously tied to the idiosyncratic spaces that read as dramatic exterior sculpture. The danger is not that Gehry cannot handle this transitional, boundary-crossing form superbly—he is the first of those who have embraced "organic" or "free form" design to make it work as architecture—but that he could be seduced by popular acclaim and prodigious publicity into a spectacular stylistic formalism. There is no doubt that he searches for his solutions as diligently and conscientiously as ever; as one revelatory design follows another, there is no diminution of creative energy, no less thoughtful pursuit of the right forms for the purpose. Each new building breaks new ground. The branch of New York's Guggenheim Museum in Bilbao, Spain (1993–1997), achieves a extraordinary level of invention and art. The eccentric shapes, like sails on the harbor, are all computer-analyzed in complex, three-dimensional detail; the configurations are exactly calculated for engineering material and cost.

Christian de Portzamparc's work is in a totally different idiom; in photographs it can be easily dismissed as consummate French chic. He likes tile, aluminum, curves, cones, and the amoeboid shapes and candy colors of 1950s modernist pop, but this enthusiasm for the motifs and mannerisms of a recent past that he is too young to really remember is subjected to a rigor and finesse that turn what could easily be camp into high Gallic style. What his buildings sometimes lack in finish comes from the pitfalls of France's two-tier construction system; since the government and the architect's office share the production of working drawings on all competition-winning public designs, details and finishes inevitably fall through the budgetary and bureaucratic cracks. But even these obvious construction flaws fail to destroy the aesthetic resolution of the building's parts.

To dismiss this work as theater, or to call it a younger generation's appropriation of near-history for its popular nostalgic and decorative appeal, one must overlook the logic and originality of Portzamparc's plans, the expert and effective way in which his solutions flow and function, his sure grasp of scale and proportion, superior sense of urban amenity, and lyrical use of light and color. In addition to Miami-modern redux, there are echoes of Oscar Niemeyer's and Roberto Burle-Marx's undulating curves that transformed Corbusian austerity into Latin American exuberance forty years ago. (Similar echoes, in a different kind of transformation, appear an ocean and two coasts away in the California work of Frank Israel.) Portzamparc clearly loves it all, without condescension. Given cultural distance and a European perspective, these sources become more than fashionable sentimentalism; he takes serious high camp into the realm of serious high art. This is the kind of serious hedonism that the French do so well.

Make no mistake, this is serious architecture as well as profound French chic. But unlike so much French architecture, where the chic is skin-deep, Portzamparc's is innovative work with an impressive range of dramatic invention. Only a seriously assured architect could carry it off. It does not hurt his growing reputation that he has the appealing look of a star-crossed rather than a star architect. Nor is he alone in the persistent incorporation of personal stylistic icons; James Stirling had his lighthouses, and Aldo Rossi has those cabanas and haunting skeletal stairs.

The promenade that circles Christian de Portzamparc's concert hall at the Cité de la Musique in Paris, *right,* leads to the theater's entrance, studios, a museum, and eventually, to the street. The curving path that never reveals what lies beyond and subtle changes in light and color enrich the processional act. *Photo, Nicolas Borel.*

Portzamparc has built an impressive number of structures in Paris that include the monumental Cité de la Musique at La Villette and the Dance School of the Paris Opera in the suburb of Nanterre. The Cité de la Musique, a competition-winning design of 1983 that took a decade to complete, is part of one of Mitterrand's *grands travaux* and one of the better achievements to come out of that imperial effort.[17] This major cultural project consists of two large buildings on the edge of the Parc de la Villette with a plaza between them: a national conservatory of music and dance, with classrooms and performance facilities in one, and a major new concert hall, with connecting studios and a museum in the other. One is never aware that the conservatory is partly underground; the entrance from the street leads into a multistory space with a top-to-bottom view of the interior from a central stair; tiered, open balconies function as exterior corridors on all floors. This entire space is flooded with natural light from large glass walls at ground level and above. The glass walls look out on amazing vistas—across to a cone-shaped organ recital hall or up to an undulating canopy pierced by a huge oculus through which one sees the sky. Quiet, soundproof areas adjoin open, public spaces in a plan that skillfully relates study and social uses. Art deco railings, stylish furniture, and beguiling colors banish any institutional air.

The concert hall starts with a stunning public act. Visitors arriving from the park, the street, or the conservatory across the plaza step down into a roofed but open court that serves as a collecting point for pedestrian traffic; this movement is then channeled along a curving, covered promenade leading to and circling the concert hall. In no way is this a traditional promenade in the City Beautiful sense; choreographed as much as designed, it relies on the drama and mystery of movement as well as on traditional monumental scale and architectural form. The space is intriguingly ambiguous in its covered/open, public/private nature and in the circular path that never quite reveals what lies beyond. One can enter the hall or proceed to the studios and museum; continuing on, the corridor exits to the street. As the corridor unfolds, the curving path narrows toward its end and the walls change in hue; Portzamparc is also a painter with an artist's eye for what color does to a place and the people in it. Inside the large concert hall, one of numerous performance and practice spaces on which Pierre Boulez was an active

17 Djamila Mefti, *Les grands travaux sous François Mitterrand, 1981–1991* (Monaco: Editions du Rocher, 1991).

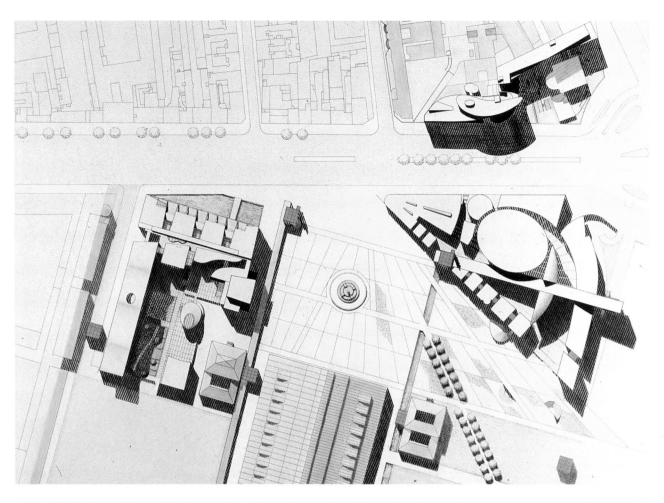

The Cité de la Musique in Paris's Parc de la Villette. Exterior views of the Conservatory, *top and bottom, left;* entrance lounge, *bottom, right.*

The plan, *opposite page, top,* shows me a conservatory with classrooms and performance spaces on the left, the concert hall with studios and museum on the right. Each structure is a collection of individual units containing specific functions, connected by circulation routes. *Bottom,* The organ cone of the conservatory, *Photos, Nicolas Borel.*

collaborator, a rainbow of colored lights can instantly imbue the handsome wood panels with Hollywood glamour, a feature dear to the architect's heart.

Portzamparc's Dance School of the Paris Opera in Nanterre (1983–1987) is also a competition-winning design; all public projects in France go through this route. The building is quite literally the sum of its individual parts: the dance studios, an administration and classroom area, and student dormitories. A glass-walled entrance leads to all three sections; the plan is shaped by circulation patterns based on the acoustic isolation of the studios, the social orientation of classrooms and offices, and the privacy of the dormitories, which are housed in a serpentine wing that curves across the landscape like a tail. The building's focus is a dramatic, full-height, helicoidal stair that unites the dance studios on all levels. This central circulation space is open, with constantly visible movement up and down the stairs and along the mezzanines that alternate with the studio entrances on different floors. Connecting bridges across this central space become small lounges that tie the activities together and provide a place for the dance students to pause between them. Like the art it is designed for, the building has an airy grace.

Portzamparc is both a sophisticated stylist and a sensitive urbanist, concerns that are usually considered antithetical. He moves easily between scales, handling the bold monumentality of the Cité de la Musique and the subtleties of a small addition to Paris's Bourdelle Museum (1988–1992) with equal expertise. The museum's pale gray, textured plaster walls are gently washed with diffused daylight that opens and softens the too confining galleries overfilled with heroic sculpture that seems to barge about. Occasionally he goes blissfully overboard, proudly presenting an oddball, boomerang-shaped solution to a less-than-tuned-in audience. He is not immune to the unremitting French fascination with Googie, the 1950s modernism of diners and filling stations where a campy outrageousness now passes for inspired originality. But he has something that other architects recognize instantly, the single-minded application of a poetic creativity of rich dimensions. His best buildings succeed not only because of his basic architectural skills, but also because they address fundamental concerns: the needs and pleasures of the body and the spirit, those human values which all great architecture serves and turns into art.

Color studies for the walls of the concert hall building, *top;* the concert hall, *Bottom.*

The three sections of Portzamparc's Dance School for the Paris Opera at Nanterre are separated for administration, classrooms, and a student dormitory. A high, glass-walled entrance, *top,* that serves them all, is set back from the long, articulated facade, *bottom. Photos, Stephane Couturier.*

The dramatic focus of the Dance School is a sweeping, skylit spiral stair connecting studios on every level. *Photo,* Von Robaye. The plan, *bottom,* emphasizes the privacy of the tail-like dormitory wing. *Photo,* Steve Morez.

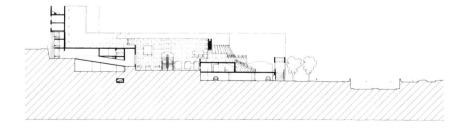

Conclusions

An age of form givers—those giants of the earlier twentieth
century, Le Corbusier, Mies van der Rohe, Frank Lloyd Wright,
with everyone else working in their shadow—has been followed by
a flowering of many talents on an unprecedented scale. These architects are carrying the earlier revolutionary achievements to another
level of the building art. What is common to all is the process of
design. Architecture is no longer conceived as the making of a
formal "container," as it developed over centuries of stylistic evolution. Modernism "broke the box," piercing the walls and moving
the volumes about; the new work explodes the last restrictive
formal geometry. Architects today think first in terms of interior
space and how it works, and second in terms of enclosure; they
begin by studying a building's component parts for a searching
analysis of their rationale. Functions are not merely assigned to
certain spaces; they are given conceptual and visual identity and
shaped freely and imaginatively, with often striking results.

Buildings have ceased to be boxes with membranes defining indoor
and outdoor domains. Their spaces are no longer conceived as static,
finite enclosures but as serial and open-ended. The significance of
this approach is that the building's elements can be redesigned and
reassembled in a variety of unconventional configurations, with a
greater consciousness—and, sometimes, radical interpretation—
of the relationship of use and form. The parts become the whole
through a great variety of integrating ideas and devices; ramps,
bridges, and spaces perceived on more than one plane or level, transparent or translucent walls and divisions, carefully programmed or
eliminated visual barriers, the use of light for subtle games of now
you see it, now you don't—all add elements of enrichment or
surprise. Circulation holds it together; movement through the
building is an important design factor.

The exterior enclosure of these new arrangements becomes a free
exercise in style and a matter of personal preference in this time of
pluralistic taste and expression. This freedom, rather than chaos in
the profession or competing claims of correctness, explains much of
the diversity of today's production. Far more important is the
expansion of the art of architecture itself; to its conventional definition as a three-dimensional, spatial art a fourth dimension has been
added: an aesthetic of time-related experiences and effects.
Interlocking, layered views are seen simultaneously and sequen-
tially. The eye and the body are invited and often required to
register perceptions and sensations of an actual and aesthetic

complexity rarely encountered before. John Hollander has defined architectural genius as "the ability to conceive new relations between beauty and use and to change forever something — however small—about the nature of the realm of enclosed space."[1] Both the vision and the reality of architecture are quite literally changing the way we see and use buildings.

All of this work must be visited personally; what one sees in pictures are the strange shapes and stylistic mannerisms that merely hint at the strategies beneath. Gehry's eccentric piles of richly colored sculptural shapes may seem arbitrary or oblivious to the basic laws of gravity and order, but this is a precisely calibrated disorder, sedulously studied and arranged. What he is pursuing is a fundamental investigation of the art of building and the new forms this may take. Portzamparc invokes 1950s imagery with unabashed élan, but this artful nostalgia serves a skilled functional and social organization infused with light and color. Siza's work is the most abstract: it depends on the exacting organization of its minimal components, resolving complex needs in forms of absolute, elemental purity. It has immense poetic rigor and is the hardest to imitate. No one has yet surpassed Stirling's brilliant, original synthesis of past and present. As striking as the differences among these gifted practitioners is the similarity of their methods and objectives. This is an art moving to fresh solutions, as it bypasses a stagnant, dead-ended postmodernism and a warped traditional revival that is already proving itself unreal, thin, and dry. It is creative change of this magnitude that defines the history of art.

No matter how original or idiosyncratic, however, none of this new work is immaculately conceived. Architecture is a creative continuum; it is self-referential, building on its own experience even when it seems to break with it. The cumulative architectural heritage underlies even the most radical change. Like poetry, John Hollander tells us, "Architecture is…in some way, always 'about' itself…There is no way out—for the architect as for the poet—of confronting the history of the art."[2] While the common source today is an assimilated and transformed modernism, the new architecture has deeply embedded references to the past. The result is as different from the earlier modernist architecture of this century, or the architecture of any other century, as changes in

1 HOLLANDER, op. cit., 33.

2 Ibid., 31.

society, life, and thought can make it. What remains constant and unchanging is the difficult, essential, and artful resolution of those basic things with which architects must always deal—structure, space, form, and light—and all of the pragmatic and poetic input of a humanistic art, for human needs, shaped by a personal vision and the common culture.

This kind of architectural change is not an instinctive or unpremeditated act. All architects seek some kind of belief or ideology, an intellectual rationale to support ideas that break through custom to explore new kinds of vision and design, to find new definitions of art and use. The objective is discovery, or the reconstitution of the familiar in a freshly revealing way, something that enlarges experience and heightens sensibility and, ultimately, creates a greater conceptual and aesthetic range. Ideas are instruments of great power and persuasion; they alter art and history. They change our perception and understanding of the world around us. Architecture deals in these conspicuously altered states.

But this is an art in which theory plays a peculiarly ambiguous and problematic role. Architects are coattail philosophers, adopting and bowdlerizing intellectual trends as they go out of style. Today's literary and philosophical borrowings, force-fed into a pragmatic, problem-solving art, become, at most, barely recognizable and, at worst, destructively irrelevant. Theory can redefine or derail architecture, and much of today's transposed and misused literary and linguistic philosophy is inherently and inescapably antiarchitectural. Drawings of baffling beauty and stupefying complexity remain unbuilt, and buildings that look as if they are falling down or flying apart achieve that effect only by being as carefully put together as Palladian villas. What one admires and accepts about the more arcane theoretical work depends a great deal on one's dedication to the new and inscrutable, and on personal levels of architectural masochism. Spectacular images can bring equally spectacular dysfunction. For better or worse, however, nothing guarantees a four-star architectural attraction quite like a dose of revolutionary obscurantism, and there is little that is more seductively appealing to the young than being terminally iconoclastic. Architecture is not immune to the lure of celebrity and shock value in a society that cultivates the new and novel at any cost.

The one perennial, legitimate, philosophical debate about this complex art has always been, and will continue to be, about art versus use, vision versus pragmatism, theory versus reality, aesthetics versus social responsibility. These unavoidable conflicts are unique to the art of architecture; they provide its essential and productive tensions; they challenge talent and force solutions. The tragedy is that so little rises above the leveling off imposed by compromise. The form in which those solutions are cast is a response to the many cultural and societal factors that determine style. Style is what we are, at any time; it is how art expresses and gives meaning to our tastes, needs, and convictions, to the way we think and act, to what we believe we are and hope to be. There is no architecture, no beauty, no art, without style. But ultimately, it is not the way something looks, or how that look is achieved, that is of primary importance. What matters is what it does, whether we receive that extra dimension of dignity or delight and elevated sense of self that the art of building can provide through the nature of the places in which we live and work.

Nor is the architect any stranger to illusion; the entertainment industry has no exclusive franchise on special effects. Illusion is one of architecture's most ancient and potent tools. To create places that dignify, inspire and uplift, transform and delight, far beyond their capacity to shelter and serve, requires more than strict attention to materials and construction. Beyond its tangible, corporeal, pragmatic presence, architecture *is* illusion. But what the architect delivers is no fast fix; this is illusion performed at the highest level of art, since "the whole realm of interior and exterior space is one of poetic fiction as well as of contrived experience."[3] Architecture conjures transforming, timeless structures out of a legal outline on the ground; it turns the air above that restrictive and arbitrary perimeter into forms, spaces, and enclosures that must exist fully in the architect's imagination before they acquire any substance at all. Nothingness is transformed into enduring images. Architecture is illusion as reality.

Whatever its stated purposes, architecture has always sought memorable images: Brunelleschi's cathedral dome dominates Florence; Bernini's embracing plaza defines St. Peter's and Rome. A Borromini chapel curves and spirals to a climax in a frescoed cupola that elevates worship to wonder; our continuing reverence and

3 J. HOLLANDER, Ibid., p.30.

response do not depend on the original religious impulse that inspired it. After modernism's rigid insistence that form follow function, architects have rediscovered that a stair is more than a way to get from one place to another; it can be a stage, an indicator of social and cultural hierarchies, a subtle transition, or a roll of thunder. Symbol and metaphor are as much a part of the architectural vocabulary as stone and steel.

Cities grow out of wilderness through controlling acts of design. The serene classicism of Washington, D.C., replaced a swamp. Consider London's intimate green squares; think of the city without them. Rome would be something else and something less, deprived of the scale and splendor of its plazas and fountains. The ideal vision of the Renaissance city endures in perspectival Italian vistas lined with palazzi. The supreme elegance of Paris came not from some natural force; it is a product of the taste and power of its builders—kings, architects, and engineers. Le Nôtre turned virgin forest into the pomp and splendor of Versailles's *grandes allées.* Those Old World towns that attract and charm us may be serendipitous in their form and growth, but their enchantment comes from a style, or series of styles, that have existed over time and created their special character.

The nature of public places, of investment-generated grids, even of speculative chaos, is something imposed on the land by accident or will, by design or default. But all are settings to which we respond—to which, in fact, we are captive. We have no choice; the result, life-diminishing or life-enhancing, is inescapable. Physical and spiritual needs must still be satisfied while complying with complex laws and codes, shifting economics and politics, public or private agendas. To turn these conflicting factors into construction that is more than a minimal container or bottom-line investment is not only a formidable challenge, it is illusion of a very special sort.

It was not until our own day that this great art became irrelevant, that the tradition of building well ceased to matter. For those in positions of power, architecture has no redeeming value; it is a frill to be eliminated as a virtuous, cost-cutting, vote-getting measure; it can be abandoned without regret. It took today's mean mentality to see cathedrals and courthouses as "waste space," to consider beauty as an extravagant and expendible add-on; only now has that impoverishment of the human spirit become politically and aesthetically correct. What no one appears to have noticed, while deploring the decline of public standards, is that trashy buildings trash the institutions and people they serve. Many factors have created disrespect for our legal system; but the act of dispensing justice from sleazy, jerry-built courtrooms of bargain-basement tackiness declares that there is no majesty or justice in the law. The great orders of Greece, the noble arches of Rome, the soaring vaulting and buttressed and carved stone of medieval cathedrals, the dramatic, illusory spaces of the Baroque, speak to more than a roof and walls; each style, in its own way, addressed and answered human and societal needs that architecture alone can fill. The skylit rotundas and ceremonial spaces of our own colonnaded and crested nineteenth-century public buildings were meant to embody and share commonly held values and ideals of democracy and the prestige and power of the state. Illusion, all, of course. But these are the illusions we have lived by.

Illusion is now retronostalgia, schlock substitutes, themed parodies, from Las Vegas's eye- and mind-boggling spectacles to the slick, simplistic commercial and entertainment caricatures that cheapen and diminish their plundered sources. Today everything seems to conspire to reduce life and feeling to the most deprived and demeaning bottom line. But it still matters—perhaps more than ever in this time of the shoddy, the transient, and the unreal—whether or not architecture improves our experience of the built world, whether it makes us wonder why we never noticed places in quite this special, affecting way before, or whether it condemns us to its own low level, stripped of all the values and content held through time. The test, finally, goes beyond any battle of the styles; it is the manner in which ideas, vocabulary, and structure are employed; how far these instruments of exploration carry architecture into new areas of use and sensory satisfaction; how well they move building beyond current limitations; whether that work serves and satisfies us, in the personal and much larger societal sense; and, ultimately, how this process engages and reveals necessity and beauty in the language of our time.

It is a curious trick of history and fate that the gap between the real world of architecture and the synthetic world of mass-marketed substitutes has never been so great as it is now—that it is virtually unbridgeable, without middle ground. The marvels of reproduction made possible by modern technology and mass production and marketing have given us the "almost real," the "near-perfect," and the "authentic reproduction" as objects of wonder and desire that everyone can possess. The word "artificial," once used to distinguish the real thing from the imitation, has lost its edge. Architecture itself is divided into two camps: those for whom kitsch is king, who endow popular culture with some cosmic creative significance beyond its legitimate role and place; and those engaged in the pursuit of the most hermetic philosophical and arcane rationales for an increasingly esoteric and disconnected art. Both have lost interest in architecture's larger public role and social responsibility. Both have substituted labored and distorted readings for the direct responses that architecture has always evoked.

In the real world, pop art and high art not only coexist but also are equal partners in a complex environment made far more interesting and useful by the mix. Nor must "high" be alien or inaccessible. Architecture is an immediate, personal, one-on-one experience. "Light and spaciousness are not acquired tastes," the critic Herbert Muschamp has observed, writing of Richard Meier's Swissair building. This pristine white structure, just off the Long Island Expressway, conspicuously lacks the pop signs and symbols meant to impress the motorist that were immortalized by the Venturis' treatises on the subject. "Swissair and White Castle aren't polar opposites," Muschamp points out. "A finely tuned glass wall rising from a green lawn gives as much pleasure to people who may never have heard of Le Corbusier as it does to those who enjoy parading their erudition. . . .good books sometimes make the best-seller list, great movies have found audiences, and some architects have always fought to operate intelligently in the popular sphere."[14]

The public sphere is having a tough time of it, as the private preserves of theme park and supermall increasingly substitute for nature and the public realm, while nostalgia for what never was replaces the genuine urban survival.

It will no longer be necessary to travel the extra miles to the ocean for the Key West experience when the main (read "entertainment") features of this unique Florida environment are reproduced inland at Orlando. The *USF Constellation* in Baltimore's Inner Harbor, a frigate built in 1797 and long advertised as the oldest warship afloat, turns out to be a replica, completely rebuilt in the 1850s, according

14 HERBERT MUSCHAMP, "A Reason to Rubberneck on the Expressway," *New York Times*, February 26, 1995.

to the navy's curator of ship models. "So it wasn't the original one, so what?" was a visitor's response. "How many things in life are original anyway?"

Gresham's law may apply, as the meretricious drives out the genuine, but the art of architecture gives every sign that it will endure. Architects are a tough, idealistic breed who insist on entering a field where monetary rewards are low and risks and obstacles are high, but where the visions, when realized, can change the world. They practice "an ancient art, once known as the mother art," Muschamp reminds us, "because it provided the public, physical framework for the development of civilization."[5] This is no Mickey Mouse agenda. Whatever junk can do, the real thing can do better. Against all odds—and the odds are increasing—architecture will always be the mother art that shapes our cities and our lives.

5 HERBERT MUSCHAMP, "A Victim of a Malady It Tried to Diagnose," *New York Times*, January 21, 1996.

Index